THE DIAMOND
Second Edition

Books by Bobby Owens

Enlisted Leadership Laboratory

- **The Star and the Wreath**
  ISBN: 1-884308-21-X

- **Platoon Sergeant**
  ISBN: 1-884308-04-X

- **Squad Leader**
  ISBN: 1-884308-06-6

- **The Gray Area**
  ISBN: 1-884308-35-X

- **The First Sergeant ... an introduction**
  ISBN: 1-884308-26-0

- **The Command Sergeant Major ...**
  An Introduction
  ISBN: 1-884308-28-7

- **The First Sergeant Spouse Notes**
  ISBN: 1-884308-27-9

- **The Command Sergeant Major**
  Spouse Notes
  ISBN: 1-884308-25-2

THE DIAMOND
Second Edition

The Power behind the Throne

Command Sergeant Major (Ret) Bobby Owens

To order additional copies of this book, contact:
Xlibris Corporation
1-888-795-4274
www.Xlibris.com
Orders@Xlibris.com
34170

CONTENTS

◊ ◊ ◊ ◊ ◊ ◊ ◊ ◊ ◊ ◊ THE DIAMOND ◊ ◊ ◊ ◊ ◊ ◊ ◊ ◊ ◊ ◊

Second Edition

YOUR OWNERSHIP PAGE

NAME:

SSAN:

DOB:

SPOUSE'S NAME:

QUALIFICATIONS/SPECIAL SKILLS:

CHILDREN'S NAMES: _____

_____

_____

RELIGION:

PERMANENT HOME ADDRESS:

EDUCATION:

DEDICATION: I, _____ dedicate this

book to my beloved _____ on this

_____day of _____ (year) _____.

FIRST SERGEANT'S COURSE:

CLASS NUMBER:

AWARDS/DECORATIONS:

THE DIAMOND

The Diamond was the mark of me.
       An old country person with big ideas you see.
       Before the days of "Be All That You Can Be."

The Diamond was the mark of me.
       Knew it from the very start

To be a top sergeant in the greatest Army.
       Known to every part—especially my heart.

The Diamond was the mark of me.
       Its shape made me stand.
One voice said you will never get to wear it.
       Another said—yes, you can.

The Diamond was the mark of me.
       Not the Power that I would seek.
Just got to wear that diamond.
       A symbol not meant for the meek.

The Diamond was the mark of me.
       With it to lead the way.
To salute all the great soldiers,
       With whom I served yesterday and serve today.

The Diamond was the mark of me.
       Passing from follower to top leader.
I knew that it would be mine.
       A point I didn't long have to consider.

The Diamond was the mark of me.
>To influence and direct.
To share with my soldiers the sadness and sorrow.
>To do all within my power to maintain their loyal respect.

Then I was a first sergeant with my ever extended day.
>Seemed as if it was always work and never play.
To look a platoon sergeant straight in the eye and say—
>"This is the way."
The Diamond was the mark of me.

The Diamond is the greatest position to hold.
>In all contact it has shown.
Though the Star and the Wreath is greater, I am told.
>But for now, "I am the power behind the throne."

Bobby Owens

PREFACE

The Byzantines believed that their Emperor derived his authority from God. Therefore he had to be obeyed. The Emperor made laws, and commanded the Army and Navy. The Emperor also supervised trade and industry. Generally, he chose the man who would succeed him to the throne.

First Sergeant, we are not Byzantine Emperors. When Byzantine mentalities develop, we must realize from whence comes our power as Noncommissioned Officers. The diamond is a symbol of service to those we supervise.

You first sergeants are the nest of experienced individuals whose professional abilities must match all your ambitions. You have got to be willing, as well as able, to make personal contributions to the advancement of those who will some day replace you. You must develop a comprehensive knowledge of the military systems and how they function.

Preparing Mentally for the Position: Premeditated mental activation is not waiting until, by some act of faith, a first sergeant pins on the diamond, thus beginning a thought process of understanding the magnitude of the job. At this point, not preparing mentally is not an irreparably destructive factor. However, by completing the premeditated mental activation, you will be that much better prepared to accomplish the task at hand, which requires a submission of will to be the best first sergeant who has ever worn the "Diamond." You must strive not to be one who just does his or her "first sergeant time." You also must carry the message that there is no such thing as "first sergeant's time."

TRAINING SHORTFALL ...

Service schools do not teach many of the essential leadership management and social techniques that are particularly appropriate concerning the duties and actions, and the moral, legal or mental accountability of a first sergeant. These are time-proven experiences that support the fact that first sergeants are grown (developed from experience).

A first sergeant is truly experienced at the two-year mark and should be highly effective, having gone through his or her growing pains. Much of what has to be learned has been learned at the two-year mark. The first sergeant then really fine-tunes his or her performancing, correcting all the interrelated principles and procedures. At this point, all who come in contact with the first sergeant can readily observe that highest level of confidence.

At the height of his or her effectiveness, generally at the two-year mark, most first sergeants look to make a move to another position. At that point, the diamond leadership cycle starts over and the soldiers are subjected to the growing pains of the new person wearing the diamond. This is one of the reasons the first sergeant must work harder than anyone else in the chain to train someone to replace him or her—good NCO-DP for platoon sergeants. The company's NCO-DP program must focus on how you best can prepare platoon sergeants to be first sergeants. At the present time, the systems wait until he or she is selected for the position or until he or she is a first sergeant, before presenting the institutional training.

Having stated that problem, I will note that this book is not designed to train first sergeants to be first sergeants. The intent is to help with the transitional growing pains, speed up the effectiveness process, and raise the confidence level while influencing and directing soldiers. The responsibilities and duties in this time-honored position of first sergeant should receive the system's full attention. The full effect and influence that you, as the first sergeant, will have on soldiers will not be realized by the soldiers until long after you have left the scene of diamond action.

Confusion has always existed among Noncommissioned Officers concerning first sergeants' duties, authority, and responsibilities and how these elements are intertwined with Commissioned Officers' duties and responsibilities. This book will assist in clarifying to some extent the duties and responsibilities for the position of the first sergeant.

Whereas the duties and responsibilities of the first sergeant cannot be described in detail because they vary among organizations, there are some techniques and principles common to the position, and it is on those aspects does this book dwell and reflect.

> . . . Learn, grow, set standards, and achieve them, create and innovate, take prudent risks, never settle for less than the best. Committed to excellence.
>
> AR 623-205 • 15 May 2002

INTRODUCTION

Commanders are not normally expected to have an expanded knowledge of the diamond wearer's implied duties. Knowing the diamond wearers' responsibilities and requirements will facilitate the commander's ability to command. In time and with experience the commander will realize that many of these implied tasks are derived from the commander's own specified duties, responsibilities or requirements. The first sergeant allocates time and coordinates learning opportunities with the commander for development purposes. Someday this commander will be a senior leader, who will need to understand the implied task's agenda of an enlisted soldier. New commanders often come to the job thinking that the first sergeant is awaiting their directives before any actions are initiated. The diamond wearer must quickly educate the new commander by explaining the interconnection of their duties, requirements and responsibilities.

Enlightened first sergeants know that the shroud of mystique that embodies the noncommissioned officer corps can never be completely explained to the commissioned officer corps. The diamond wearer must take every opportunity to train, coach, mentor and develop the members of the unit. A great deal of information about the enlisted implied tasks' agenda can be ingested by the commander in bits and pieces from the diamond wearer. The commander must understand above all else how the duties, requirements, and responsibilities of the command team interact in support of each other's role requirements.

. . . two-way dependency . . .

It is the first sergeant's responsibility to ensure that the commander understands that by allowing him or her the freedom to execute the implied tasks agenda does not reduce any of the commander's command authority. Actually, it is enhanced. It must be explained to the commander that it is a two-way dependency when the first sergeant's years of experience are relied upon to maintain the routine of the military routine. Such simple military procedures (chapter action, flagging soldier records, NCOERs,

13

etc.), are often seen as too complicated and difficult. The diamond wearer's ability allows the faster review of NCOERs rather than someone trying to compare NCOER to AR 623-205 while reviewing it. Therefore, the diamond wearer is relied upon by the commander and the units' leadership groups to prevent the routines from becoming complicated.

... understanding the contents ...

The first sergeant attuned to the requirements of the unit guides the officers in understanding the contents of the noncommissioned officer's implied tasks agenda. In addition to derive developmental benefits that results from the interaction between the two corps, it also projects the idea that the noncommissioned officer, to a great degree, is in control of individual training tasks and self-development efforts. It is a statement that the required assessment of the soldier's proficiency level has been made and the required follow-on training is being incorporated into the long range planning. It is also a statement that the quality of collective training will only be realized if the noncommissioned officers are allowed to execute the implied training tasks portion of their implied tasks agenda. The contents of the noncommissioned officer's implied tasks agenda does not embrace any mysticism.

The first sergeant possess the skills that underpin attributes that characterize the diamond wearer's ability to facilitate planning the unit's efficiency. What is more important is that it provides purpose and motivates several different levels of soldier's development. Just how does the diamond wearer do this? He or she does this by conducting a series of positive activities. These activities seek to engender cooperation, expediency, integrity, consistency, and efficiency. They promote other skills needed to enhance the unit's performance. While demonstrating solidarity and professional balance, the diamond wearer creates courses and seminars designed to help officers to understand the contents of the noncommissioned officer's implied agenda.

There is no enlisted leadership position in the Army that is more rewarding and influencing than that of the first sergeant's position. The first sergeant's position interpersonal requirements are so much more extensive than those of other enlisted leadership positions. It is the diamond wearer who transforms the enlisted leadership interpersonal inputs which characterizes the basic leadership process. The wearer establishes the content in which the enlisted leadership groups must operate. Then it is the wearer who attaches meaning to these interpersonal inputs for the officers.

It is the enlightened diamond wearer who exerts that powerful positive influence. He or she provides stability, regulates behaviors to conform, fastens proficiency, challenges everyone to grow and develop (ensures future availability of competent leaders), and selects unit personnel for professional development courses. Anything that tears at the proficiency, morale, operational, the esprit-de-corps, or administrative fabric of the unit are in direct conflict with the diamond wearer. The commander and the wearers are the central figures in the unit. The requirements for competency, the obligation to adhere to standards and the spirit of disciplines to share hardships and successes, and to sustain the conditions for trust are but a few of the items that must be embraced. If these things were understood by the members of the unit, conflict would be minimized. These are the elements or the strands that hold the inner unit together.

The diamond wearer's burden is to do all within the wearer's power to increase the likelihood that the unit's leadership groups will adopt and internalize the values' systems. It reduces the need to punish, control or to demand compliance and highlights the interpersonal methods required to be performed as part of this enlightened leadership position.

The wearer makes common unit experiences as widespread as possible so that all who are exposed to similar challenges (as part of the development structure) benefits from the exposure (lessons learned). Enlightened future enlisted leaders will come forth from units with enlightened diamond wearers.

There is no book that could be written that could enumerate or encompass the diamond wearer's awesome abilities to positively influence all those who come in contact with them. Success hinges a great deal on the commander acknowledging that the diamond wearer is the unit's catalyst. It is the first sergeant who creates a spark when or where there is none, establishing or developing when required, attacking and or praising to accommodate the situation. The diamond wearer's position is a vast collection of books: field manuals, technical manuals, Department of Defense Regulations, Reserve Regulations, Guards Regulations, Army Regulations, other military publications, and civilian publications. They support the diamond wearer's efforts to complete required doing tasks

(DTs), direct supervising and supporting tasks (DSSTs) and the follow-on supervising and support tasks (FSSTs).

The diamond wearer over the course of a career commits much of this information to memory. However, the wearer maintains a library to assist in the performance of the mentoring requirements. The regulation mandates that copies of AR 623-205 be made available to the noncommissioned officers supported by copies maintained by the wearer.

—The Diamond Theme—

"The diamond wearer's competency skills
must be developed and practiced long before the wearer
assumes this position of great responsibility."

CHAPTER I

SELECTION

> A diamond is a chunk of coal
> that made good under pressure.

INTRODUCTION:

The changing face of war poses special challenges for the senior enlisted leaders, especially at the first sergeant and sergeant major levels. The new capacities to wage war by those hostile to democracy requires your individual and collective attention. The best way the U.S. can have a reasonable chance of staying out of war is to maintain a military force in sufficient numbers, and with professionalism among the noncommissioned officer corps.

The supreme value of our warfighting proficiency is that it will give us teams that will be able to operate independently of the parent unit, while still performing missions with the overall intent of the commander. How do we get there? We get there by having forward-thinking senior enlisted soldiers who want to be a part of molding and developing our future Army. The key person to this warfighting proficiency is the first sergeant.

Complex Leadership:

   ... complex leadership created ...

Social changes and technological changes that have produced highly lethal weapon systems also have created the requirement for complex leadership roles for our future enlisted leaders. Therefore, our systems and methods of learning must keep pace with these technological changes so that our leaders can achieve their full potential as soon as possible. Therefore, we need to take a hard, cold look at how our junior leaders at the organizational level are thrust into their new roles as trainers. The "Diamond" is designed to present the future position holders with somewhat of a broad map to ensure the effectiveness of the force. That effectiveness is pushed to the lowest levels of leadership.

Without quality-trained enlisted leaders, ones who are trained to train, our sophisticated and advanced technological equipment becomes antiquated. Leaders trained to train are combat multipliers. You cannot be negligent in fulfilling perhaps the one most important responsibility—that of ensuring that future leaders and soldiers are trained in the arts of war.

First Sergeant, you have got to stress to the NCO corps, every day that you breathe, that professional job competence (technical and tactical proficiency) is an absolute prerequisite to developing the framework for leadership in your unit.

POSITION OF SERVITUDE . . .

. . . the noblest creature . . .

The first sergeant position, as are all positions of leadership, is a position from which one's subordinates are to be served. If your reasons for being a first sergeant are anything other than to serve, then in the best interest of all concerned, especially the noblest creature on the face of the Earth, the American soldier, you should seek employment elsewhere. Foremost in your mind should be, "How will I make the noblest creature on the face of the Earth successful at what he or she is to do—fight wars?" We all can acknowledge the fact that to serve our country in the profession of arms is not easy but patriotic.

. . . protecting the noblest creature . . .

If you wish to occupy the position for any reasons other than to be the chief advocate of the soldier and his or her family, then your ship is off course. You are the one who must protect the soldier from those in leadership positions who say that they have the soldier's best interests at heart, but whose actions show otherwise. Protect soldiers from that civilian who is employed because of that soldier. Make an effort to ensure that the command work force respects soldiers. There have always been civilians who love soldiers, as demonstrated by their actions.

We have established the fact that the first sergeant position is one of service to subordinates. The first sergeant serves the subordinate by ensuring:

◊ An organizational life that is conducive to learning and professional development of every member of the unit. (Referred to as Command Climate.)

◊ Tough Training—the realities of the field of battle are not close to anything one will experience in training. The object of training is to prepare the soldier for war, and to create the understanding that the object of any enemy in war is to prevent the soldier from continuing the war.

◊ The cherishing and nourishing of the sprouting human resources we refer to as the junior leadership.

◊ That not even missions (in peace) will have such a high priority that they would rob a soldier or his or her family of dignity, nor would prevent a soldier from attending to the basic human needs.

SELECTION ...

... highly qualified and highly motivated ...

Selection and assignment of the most highly qualified and motivated senior soldiers to the first sergeant positions is outlined in AR 614-200. Important points for one considering the eventual selection and/or assignment to a first sergeant position are:

◊ Assignments must be career-enriching and must serve as professional development for soldiers in a CMF where first sergeant opportunities are available.
◊ Normally, these most highly qualified and motivated senior soldiers will not be assigned outside their CMF.
◊ Eligibility for assignment to a first sergeant's position.
◊ Acceptance or rejection of assignment as first sergeant is not a soldier's right.
◊ These most highly qualified and motivated senior soldiers will be stabilized as first sergeant for twenty four months.
◊ Repetitive assignments to first sergeant duty.
◊ The administrative action of withdrawal of the first sergeant SQI under all circumstances.

Every soldier who sees this position as a possible future duty position should study this section of AR 614-200.

Diamond Point: The counseling would read as follows: You are hereby being counseled for the violation of Section IX, AR 614-200, which reads in part, ... assigned as first sergeant based on the following:

• Outstanding qualities of leadership
• Dedication to duty
• Integrity and moral character (ethical profile)
• Professionalism
• MOS Professionalism
• Appearance and military bearing
• Physical fitness

I do not know of any enlisted soldier who does not have a rater who points to the higher levels of challenge for the soldiers he or she rates.

Any rater who maintains the DA Form 2166-8 is derelict in his or her duty if he or she does not annotate the fact that a senior soldier rejected an assignment as first sergeant.

The second diamond point in support or the lack of support for the provisions of AR 614-200 is the fact that the practice of maintaining any form of an order of merit list for selection and assignment to the first sergeant position does not exist. AR 614-200 does not require it, therefore, a list is not maintained.

These most highly qualified and motivated senior soldiers will be stabilized as first sergeant for 24 months. That statement definitely implies that the duty should not be less than 24 months. Twenty-four months is the length of time it takes to get the framework for leadership locked in and to complete the Chronological Milestone Chart for success.

. . . the interview process . . .

The civilian job's market requires a brief and concise account of one's life experiences, education, talents, etc. in the form of a résumé. The interview process requires that specific qualities be assessed and evaluated. Jobs are obtained in part based upon the applicant's ability to express and explain how the required job attributes not contained on the résumé will be accomplished. The abilities to perform and having the required skills are laid out at the time of the interview. The truth is that the civilian job market wants to confirm the actual personal qualities, skills and knowledge that the interviewee has up front.

The military adjusts more in time with the individual's growth and development of their knowledge and experiences. The perspective candidates who don't possess the required background must demonstrate that their lack of certain skills and knowledge must not be the grounds for denial but for growth. Therefore, the military interviewer must have the right questions to identify the strengths and limitations of the position seeker. The interviewer must make a concrete and honest decision that the lack thereof (qualities) can later be acquired and reviewed.

Certain qualities are required of any position, civilian or military, but few occupations require of the individual to have as much responsibility as the military does of the first sergeant's position. The first sergeant's position is the axis around which the psychological, physical, the soldier's organizational life, family inclusions, and activities of the unit evolves and are limited. The leader interviewing a candidate must take note of certain qualities that are absolutely necessary to perform the duties and responsibilities of the first sergeant. Those sought-after qualities that may be lacking require that the leader conducting the interview take action. The interviewer must assume the responsibility and ensure that the first sergeant's development program includes methods to overcome the shortcomings identified during the interview.

. . . creating a development program . . .

Identified shortcomings so identified during the interview process provide the command sergeants major the necessary and critical insight to personally tailor the first sergeant's development program that meets all the position's requirements. The lack of a specific desired quality is not the sole justification for rejecting an otherwise most qualified soldier. The interview involves an assessment process by which personal qualities are examined. The one goal of the interview should be to seek out those lacking qualities of all the interviewed candidates. The senior leadership must then take an active role and responsibility in bringing the selected individual up to the desired standard. The senior leader conducting the interview must have and know the necessary skills, knowledge, and attitude that require senior level intervention.

. . . unit profiles . . .

The first sergeant's modus operandi upon entry into a new unit is based on the higher command's pronouncement of the units' profiles. These include the units psychological, discipline, morale, proficiency, esprit-de-corps, ethical, leadership, followship, and ethnic profiles. In addition the first sergeant must examine his or her own personal standards based on the intuitive feel for what qualities are present and must be nurtured. As the new first sergeant prepares to assume the duty position, the first sergeants' entry requires immediacy with assessment and action especially if the predecessor had problems putting a leadership agenda together. The larger and more complex the unit, the less time the new first sergeant has to assess and act. The status of the unit's profiles drives the contents of the new diamond wearer's leadership agenda.

Therefore, there is no study up period for the newly appointed first sergeant. The first sergeant must be ready to swing into action, identifying the crystal balls (the ones that can not be dropped) and the rubber balls (occasionally one can fall). The first sergeant understands that the unit's unseen psychological stability requires his or her immediate attention. The first few days of what happens or fails to happen are more critical to the wearer than to the unit. The diamond wearer in the process of assessing the unit must realize that he or she is also being assessed by the unit. The traits of leadership are on display emanating from the diamond wearer's tact, judgment, decisiveness, enthusiasm, etc. The subordinate enlisted population are developing their own mental image of how the first sergeant exercises these characteristics and traits.

... unit's internal systems ...

The unit's internal systems that identify and enhance its profiles must be assessed and the quality certified by the diamond wearer. Those systems that are within standards and in tolerance according to their design need only to be monitored. The systems that require repair should be fixed and brought back to standards. External expertise is requested by the diamond wearer for those systems that require it. The wearer knows that being too proud to request assistance is foolhardy. The wearer also redirects focus and attention from his or her position to the unit's internal systems. The wearer must never allow the unit to be subordinated to any leadership position. The outstanding qualities of the unit are the jewels in the command team's crown.

... effectiveness indicators ...

The diamond wearer equally focuses on both the objective and subjective combat effectiveness indicators to obtain as much knowledge about these two factors. This information provides the base from which the unit's guidance devices (instructions, directives, policies, classes, training planning, etc.) will emerge. The objective combat effectiveness indicators support the subjective combat effectiveness indicators with having the authorized personnel and equipment to accomplish the mission. The wearer knows that insight is gained by keeping abreast of these two significant factors. This insight will be processed until the wearer departs the unit. The wearer must know the critical personnel and equipment requirements before changes can be effected. Changes to the unit's profiles are driven by the diamond wearers understanding of these two factors.

. . . as the wheel turns . . .

The diamond wearer soon concludes that the first few weeks of the assignment are the most taxing. This is because of the intensive process of assessing, identifying, revamping, and monitoring all the internal operations of the unit. In addition, the diamond wearer also directs some of his or her attention to those systems outside the unit (the external world). All of these actions are ongoing. Family problems continue to pour in. Letters of indebtedness fill the in-box. Unit detail requirements must be planned. UCMJ actions must be completed. NCOERs are near to being late and must be completed. The list seems unending at times. Quality management and leadership are not easy, and were never meant to be. Once the wearer has a good understanding of the unit's equipment and personnel status, he or she is then better prepared. They are then able to understand and relate the morale, esprit-de-corps, the discipline, and the proficiency to determine the unit's profiles. The sound knowledge of the unit's internal operational status will lend itself to facilitating the commander's ability.

. . . hard but not insensitive . . .

The first sergeant has to be as hard as the diamond he or she wears while understanding and appreciating the beauty that draws many to want to wear the diamond. The hardness in support of the ideals that make the unit's personnel feel an attachment that always ensures that the unit's missions will be accomplished expeditiously and expediently. It is then safe to say that the first sergeant generates a kind of spirit. This spirit or attitude causes those in his or her charge to also ignite and glow with soldier power as a result of that radiating spirit from the first sergeant's personal stores.

It is the power of this diamond spirit that is able to act and react to the unit as a whole. It responds to the influencing force that affects its members. They are treated as individuals who share births, deaths, marriages, promotions, demotions, relief's, transfers, financial problems, marital problems, and personal betrayals. It also treats them as members of a collective body that have unit field exercises, tragedy involving members of the unit, sudden relief of the commander, unit award, unit inspection failure, etc.

The characteristics of the diamond also lend to further explanation in support of the qualities that must be possessed by the wearer. Its beauty must not harbor pride, prejudices, selfishness, conceit, ideas of personal gain at the expense of others, egotism, etc. The diamond wearer, foremost, takes stock of all leadership qualities that are to embody every leader in the unit including the wearer. The diamond does not exempt the wearer. It demands an additional burden of expanded trust. The wearer who camouflages herself or himself using the spirit of the diamond is among the worst of persons.

It is the spirit of the diamond that radiates a force. This force inspires, motivates, encourages, enhances, and empowers the members to share commitment, compassion and join the spirit of the diamond in most military endeavors. It is from the diamond weaver's reserves of energy and optimism that those who follow draw strength. It is from the first sergeant's spirit of the diamond that the unit personnel find inspiration. The commander too is allowed from time to time to tap this reserve of energy.

... developmental lesson in motion ...

The first sergeant's charter, as compared to the charter of other enlisted leaders, is a vast charter that contains a wide variety of unwritten duties and responsibilities. The top soldier in a unit has normally been in the service long enough to have gained much knowledge, many skills, and experiences that allow the flexibility in the first sergeant's position. The directed and specified duties must be kept to a minimum. It is from the implied duties' agenda that the developed strengths of the first sergeant are drawn.

The diamond wearer must have had a challenging developmental career up to this point. A career filled with strong mentors. Progression through the ranks that has exposed him or her to human relationship problems, environmental problems, and administrative challenges. A vast exposure to situations and circumstances that require a great deal of training management. If his or her career has been well developed by the time this soldier reaches this position, the implied tasks come naturally and with the level of confidence required of the position.

The properly functioning first sergeant is a developmental lesson in motion to all the junior enlisted soldiers desiring to attain that position. Accomplishing the mission, whatever that mission may be is all attributed to those stages through which the first sergeant has gone. The development of a first sergeant starts with a civilian transformed in thought from an individualist to one who knows the value of both individualism and collectivism. The civilian transformation to a physically and mentally well trained, well disciplined soldier is the genesis of a well rounded first sergeant.

The progression through the rank from positions of high directed and specified duties to a high implied duty's position requires that the entire education, training, and developmental base be focused. The focal point must be on producing top quality soldiers whose implied task selections are pre-enhanced by the knowledge gained at the junior leadership level. There is one valuable lesson that must be understood by the entire enlisted leadership group. The lesson is that a first sergeant who has undergone these developmental stages and understands all the growing pains is in the best position to influence the development of all subordinate leaders.

The first sergeant is the nucleus around whom the activities of the unit's enlisted corps functions. All and any actions or activities involving an enlisted soldier must involve the first sergeant. The degree of involvement is subject for discussion. That degree is determined to a large extent by the first sergeant's assessment of the subordinate leaders' abilities to accomplish the action(s). Directly or indirectly, the action will incorporate the first sergeant's DSSTs or FSSTs.

... relief from time to time ...

The myriad list of activities that a first sergeant must accomplish can be mind-staggering. He or she has to monitor, inspect, mentor, establish, revamp, assess, evaluate, manage, maintain, emphasize, plan, process, arrange, review, and investigate among other things. Despite all this, the realization is that the first sergeant is of human stuff and requires relief from time to time. To casual observers, it may seem that the diamond wearer possesses a super-human ability to withstand high levels of stress, however the first sergeant is not invincible. The experienced diamond wearer knows when to stand back with hands off with the idea of determining what functions only because of the wearer's presence and involvement. The true quality of the first sergeant lies in his or her ability to be gone and the unit or activity continues its quality operations.

The first sergeant ensures that there are trained follow-on enlisted leaders. These are leaders, who are willing to step forward and demonstrate to some degree their skills and knowledge required to manage and lead the unit. The experienced first sergeant affords these future leaders the opportunity to gain knowledge and experience as often as possible. He or she provides them with first hand experience by use of a "Hands-on" technique. The first sergeant mentors them as they "Do it." This is an integral step in the progression of developing future capable leaders.

... enumeration not required ...

The first sergeant's implied duties are not posted by the unit commander's decree. The most qualified soldier who needs the commander to enumerate implied duties should be denied the opportunity to wear the diamond. The symbol has always been entrusted to the best of the noncommissioned officer corps and it is they who composed the listing of implied tasks. Anything and everything that needs to be done at a specific time or place by specific persons for a specific reason is contained on the first sergeant's list of duties. The diamond wearer is psychologically in contact with the entire unit using the stores of collected data about the unit (combat effectiveness indicators). The wearer is a master at making the comparisons of indicators to the unit's status and should always be given the latitude to carry out the task of adjusting.

The first sergeant in essence works for the unit commander, nonetheless, the commander must allow the first sergeant to lead within the spirit of the enlisted corps. The commander who controls the duty activities of the first sergeant stifles the unit's inner spirit and at worst creates conflicts with the first sergeant. The first sergeant who finds himself or herself in such situations must explain to the unit commander that he or she can not command and be first sergeant. Commanding in itself is full-time. The first sergeant uses all the necessary respect and tact when conveying to the commander who wants to be first sergeant that the unit suffers when the commander and first sergeant can not reach an interpersonal balance. No commander wants a first sergeant to command the unit and no experienced first sergeant wants his or her commander to undermine his duties and responsibilities as the "First Sergeant."

... the spirit of the diamond ...

The spirit of the diamond is trained to engulf the psychological being of every soldier in the unit. The many years of interpersonal relationships and insights gained gives the diamond wearer that sixth-sense that enables the wearer to detect soldiers who demonstrate other than their full potential of "soldier power." It is the first sergeant who understands best that drains of individual "soldier power" diminishes the quality of the whole. Drains of "soldier power" adds up when considered in numbers. A two-hundred soldier company with low morale and skill decay pulls energy from those who are maintaining (unaffected by the element(s) causing the low morale). The first sergeant actively ensures that once this is detected, the causes for the detriment(s) are challenged. The wearer creates situations where platoon sergeants and platoon leaders quickly reach their interpersonal balance (another important subjective combat effectiveness indicator) with their peers. This includes balance within the unit as well as the surrounding units as well.

. . . cause seeking . . .

There are many reasons for the drain on "soldier power." It requires the first sergeant to demonstrate tenacity in seeking out those causes. Morale as defined by Webster is (2a: the mental and emotional condition (as of enthusiasm, confidence, or loyalty) of an individual or group with regard to the function or tasks at hand; 3: the level of individual psychological well-being based on such factors as a sense of purpose and confidence in the future). It will not always be as high as the chain of command wants it to be, however, there is a point to which it must not be allowed to fall.

. . . proficiency . . .

Proficiency, another soldier factor by which the state of the unit is measured. It is defined by Webster as the advancement in knowledge or skill. The diamond wearer's role in this process is identified, after the assessment process is completed. As the person in the unit who connects with the external world (the world outside the unit), he or she ensures that[1] the members of unit are afforded the opportunity to advance their knowledge and skills. The wearer ensures that all the unit's organic assets are used to the maximum extent to advance knowledge and skill. The wearer's focus is toward both individual and collective proficiency. Proficiency directly affects the unit's ability to accomplish each assigned mission in the highest possible standards. Skills and knowledge of the individual

---

[1]   Merriam Webster's Collegiate Dictionary, Tenth Edition

soldiers come together like all the combined material fused together in the making of a skyscraper. The diamond wearer explains to the leadership groups that morale affects attitude and that attitude affects proficiency. Low morale prevents proficiency from being completely attained and properly demonstrated. In order to properly ascertain proficiency, it has to be assessed as it is demonstrated. Easy tasks completed at minimum standards by soldiers is a sure indication that low morale is affecting proficiency. Highly proficient soldiers with high morale will always perform tasks to the highest standards when allowed to do so.

. . . discipline . . .

The diamond wearer comes armed with the knowledge that soldiers generally want their unit to be the best. Their unity and fellowship is clearly demonstrated through the forces that they are capable of influencing i.e. morale, proficiency, esprit-de-corps, discipline, etc. Discipline like proficiency is also a good indicator of unit morale level. The first sergeant keeps the leadership groups focused on the need for balancing these soldier factors. He or she ensures that the groups recognize and understand the relationship of their causes and effects. Discipline as defined by Webster is control gained by enforcing obedience or order b: orderly or prescribed conduct or pattern of behavior c: self-control. The problems in a unit are generated to some extent by the lack of discipline. This can be and at times may be a direct reflection on the first sergeant. Enforcing obedience and order or lack thereof can always spill over into the local community where soldiers go to get away from it all and where they also live. These attitudes are demonstrated by the control gained and maintained within the unit.

The enlightened first sergeant maintains the balance in the relationship of these four indicators of good leadership (morale, proficiency, esprit-de-corps, discipline). He or she is continuously observant as they are called into play as the unit performs. The first sergeant while focused on these qualities also monitors and adjusts the unit's leadership groups awareness and encourages them to do likewise. It is the diamond wearer who attunes the relationship of the four indicators within the unit and the leadership groups.

. . . uniqueness . . .

It is the first sergeant's concentrated efforts in sharing the commanders vision and communicating the intent that will cause all the unit's leadership groups to embrace it. A clearly defined goal(s) as explained by the first sergeant gives the unit its form and dictates the way they and the unit interacts. The members of the different leadership groups look to the diamond wearer to bridge those gaps between them and the commander. The first sergeant becomes the catalyst that converts unit personnel initiatives and moves the unit toward its mission accomplishments and goals. These are some of the qualities of the diamond wearer's position that gives it uniqueness.

... professional energies ...

Leadership groups focus their professional energies to some degree as directed by the diamond wearer's bearing and competence. These groups make no correlation between the selection from either the primary or secondary zone and the wearing of the diamond. In their minds there are no distinctions or attributes that selection from either zone may possibly result in failure to bring to bear skills, attitudes, and moral strengths to aid and facilitate the commander's ability to command. It is the leadership groups professional energies that are ignited by the diamond wearer's flame. This combustion then translates the individual training program into collective unit missions. The enlightened first sergeant knows that the secret to success is interlocked leadership groups. The first sergeant knows that he or she must serve them through efficient communications, and the willingness to demonstrate his or her subordination to personal needs. It is the combination of action through example by the first sergeant that ultimately cause the leadership groups do likewise and subordinate their personal needs to the needs of soldiers and mission accomplishment.

... Competence is both technical and tactical and includes reading, writing, speaking, and basic mathematics. It also includes sound judgment, ability to weigh alternatives, form objective options and make good decisions. Closely allied with competence is the constant desire to better, to listen and learn more, and to do each task completely to the best of one's ability . . . .

AR 623-205 • 15 MAY 2002

First Sergeant's Chronological Milestone

*   PrePosition Assumption Period (PPAP)
    This position requires that the senior enlisted leader, who
    knows in his or her heart that someday he or she will
    wear the "Diamond," prepare by developing a self-study
    agenda.
    (D-48 months-D24 months)
    (D-23 months-D6 months

*   Position assumption (PA)
    (D-Day?)

*   Post-Position Period (PPP)

Skills, knowledge and attitude of the diamond wearer
is demonstrated and supported by
how well the wearer actively involves himself or herself.

PrePosition Assumption Period:

The idea of these milestone charts support the idea of premeditated mental activation. You will truly be a better first sergeant if you can walk into the orderly room knowing many of the implied tasks that are being called to mind. The tasks or requirements specified here are not intended as a limit. Use them as starting points to develop effective tasks.

There is indeed a difference between the first sergeant who walks into the unit and takes six months to figure out what is going on and the first sergeant who walks in the first day and makes significant things happen (that is the essence of enlisted leadership).

Diamond Point: The characteristics of your particular unit will determine to a large degree what you should include in your framework of learning and in your framework of leadership.

If the unit has a dining facility, arms room, mail room, motor pool, or different types of equipment, then your framework should be built around what you need to learn about these operations and equipment. If you are already active (knowledgeable) in these operations, then you will be ready to execute your implied and directed tasks.

Position Assumption Period (PA):

You should not spend valuable time after you are in the position trying to determine what it is you should do first or to what degree it must be done. You should instantly put your years of experience to work formulating the plan that causes all the indicators of good leadership to rise.

Your spouse's mind must be conditioned as well for the tasks you are about to undertake. As much as possible, avoid walking into the house and announcing that you are now the first sergeant of the worst unit on post, especially if you knew months ago that you would be given the job.

First Sergeant Chronological Milestone Chart
(PrePosition Assumption)

Work To Do Before:
1.   *D-48 months to D-24 months*

    a.   Establish a framework of learning about the following:

1) Essential Management Techniques (concerning personnel, equipment, space, training)
2) Controlling mechanisms
   • coordinating • directing • evaluating
   • planning   • communicating
3) Prerequisite knowledge for cases involving nonjudicial punishment or trials by court-martial.

b   Develop your:

1) Philosophy of command and leadership.
2) Management principles.
   (Training meetings, etc.)
3) Plans for NCO events, family events.
4) Plans for conducting seminars.

c.   Discuss the occupational time requirements with your spouse. The typical day for an average-size unit is twelve hours. Also discuss a role with the Family Support Group (FSG).

d.   Consider these points:

1) How will you nourish the morale of your unit?
2) How will you promote teamwork by developing leadership qualities of subordinates?
3) How will you ensure that promotions, retirements, awards for special events, and citations for meritorious service do not go unnoticed?
4) What is it that constitutes a soldier's organizational life?
5) Why are Family Support Groups important to the unit's well-being?
6) How will you develop your platoon sergeants?
7) How do you ensure the "Warfighting Readiness" of your unit?
8) What are the pretrial confinement guidelines?
9) How will you deal with dereliction of leadership, of duty, in training?
10) How much should your spouse get involved in company social activities?

11) What is the best way to destroy "cliques" and to prevent their return?

12) How will you handle selective obedience as a disciplinary infraction?

13) Why does assessment begin the training planning process?

e. Also consider the following:

1) Why am I undertaking this critical task?

2) Do I like people or just certain people?

3) hat are management principles?

4) What are caring principles?

5) What is "Command Philosophy?"

6) What are the "Schools of Thought" concerning:

    a) Junior soldier development

    b) Recognizing family members who support unit morale efforts

    c) "The School of the Soldier"

    d) Pretrial confinement

    e) Disciplinary Infractions (minor)

    f) Social-psychological isolation

7) Why is the American soldier the noblest creature on the face of the earth?

8) What are specified, directed, and implied duties?

9) What is the concept of "ISG's Intent?"

10) Have I analyzed myself objectively?

11) What is improper command influence?

12) What is warfighting readiness?

13) When should the use of pretrial confinement be considered?

14) How much dismounted drill do I need to know?

15) Can I perform the portion of dismounted drill that the first sergeant will have to perform?

16) What part does my spouse play in this, my undertaking of leadership?

17) What are "cliques" and why are they detractors from proficiency, morale, discipline, and esprit-de-corps?
18) What is a philosopher-leader?
19) What is meant by "informal contract?"
20) What is the diamond wearer's role in the commander's training analysis (FM 25-101)?
21) How is training management information provided to the command sergeant major for the training management brief verified?
22) How does the diamond wearer project training thought in three dimensions (past, current, future)?
23) What is training thought projection (TTP)?
24) How does the diamond wearer use the results from training execution to develop training strategies?
25) Why are the unit's training strategies so important regarding those "mission essential tasks" that are not up to Army standards?
26) Why are the unit's training strategies so important when they are provided in support of the training brief given by the command sergeant major?

PrePosition Assumption Period:
D-23 months to D-6 months

a. This is by far the best period to take a high quality leave with your family to go to "stress level zero". Leave the area and relax as much as possible. You will see the need for this at about the six-month mark in the first sergeant position.
b. Define and develop good understandings of the following: (NOTE: Keep your notes used to define and develop these terms. You will need the notes to develop your subordinate leaders.)

1)	Discipline	2)	Leadership
3)	Morale	4)	Organizational life
5)	Leadership	6)	Pretrial confinement
7)	"Warrior Spirit"	8)	Dereliction
9)	Reception Program	10)	Family advocacy

11)	Preliminary inquiry	12)	Siege mentality
13)	Warfighting capability	14)	Improper command influence
15)	Dysfunctional	16)	Immoderate language
17)	Probable cause	18	Military judicial process
19)	Battlefield lethality	20)	Selective obedience
21)	Subjective combat	22)	Objective combat effectiveness indicator
23)	Training management	24)	Skill proficiency decay
25)	Multi-echelon	26)	"Warrior Spirit"
27)	Informal contract	28)	Standard enforcer
29)	Artificial dissemination	30)	Consistent mechanisms
31)	Silent cries for help	32)	nterpersonal balance
33)	Socialization	34)	Blurring of priorities
35)	Assessment		

D-5 Months to D-2 Months

a. Systems you must learn:

1) System to evaluate the methods platoon sergeants use to train their squad leaders, and a system to ensure that platoon sergeants are living up to the informal contract.
2) System that ensures that all NCOs are counseled IAW AR 623-205 and AR 600-200.
3) System to ensure that the unit SIDPERS standards are always IAW published standards.
4) System that will be used to assess the morale of the unit.
5) System for processing, controlling, and protecting the sensitive nature of DA Form 2166-8 until final processing.
6) System for processing, controlling, and protecting the sensitive nature of the DA Form 2627 (Record of Proceedings under Article 15, UCMJ).
7) System for learning the stages of the military judicial process and how the process affects the unit.
8) System for ensuring that the unit's training strategies match the unit's training deficiencies.

b. Discuss the occupational time requirements with your spouse. The typical day for an average-size unit is twelve hours. Request that your spouse read *The Command Sergeants Major Spouse Notes* by Dorothy V. Owens.

c. Study the following:

One Group	Two Group	Others
1) AR 600-20	FM 27-14	AR 600-9
2) AR 623-205	AR 640-10	AR 672-5-1
3) AR 635-200	AR 30-10	DA Form 2627
4) AR 601-280	DA Pam 608-47	AR 614-200
5) AR 600-50	DA Form 3355	
6) AR 600-200	AR 27-10	
7) AR 608-99		
8) AR 670-1		
9) DA Form 2166-8-1		
10) FM 22-5		
11) DA Form 2166-8		
12) AR 608-99		
13) FM 22-103		
14) FM 25-101		
15) Manual For Courts-Martial		
16) The First Sergeant Spouse Notes		

Position Assumption Period:
D-1 month to D-Day:

a. Interview as many of the following persons as you can:

1) First Sergeants (both active and former)
2) Company Commander (both active and former)
3) Command Sergeants Major
4) Retirees (in the above categories)
5) Staff Judge Advocate (SJA)

b. Cover the following points with the outgoing first sergeant: Prepare a list of questions about the unit, its personnel, missions, equipments, policies, chain of command, problems, shortages, trends, programs, training management status, etc.

Diamond Point: Include all aspects of both the objective and subjective combat effectiveness indicators.

1. *D + 1 to D + 14:*

    a. Familiarize yourself with the following:

        1) Mission statement (and all higher elements mission statements)
        2) Unit personnel (trends, profiles, past problems, etc.)
        3) Unit problems (trends)
        4) Past activities of the unit (good & bad)
        5) All things in the unit's file
        6) Safety program(s)
        7) Unit sponsorship program (In and Out)
        8) Unit re-enlistment
        9) Re-enlistment procedures
        10) Article 15 procedures
        11) Organizational life of your soldiers and family members

    b. Introduce yourself to the following:

        1) All of the unit's soldiers (not limited to hellos)
        2) Community support activities personnel (get to know names and operating hours)
        3) Other activities that affect morale
        4) Local chapel (for your soldiers if not for yourself)
        5) Family Support Group (FSG) (DA PAM 608-47)
        6) The Noncommissioned Officer Evaluation Reporting System Rating Chain (qualifications and special evaluation requirements).

2. *D + 15 to D + 30:*

a. Present your philosophy of command and leadership to your NCOs
b. Familiarize yourself with limitations and capabilities of your NCOs
c. Establish and introduce the following:

1) Barrack living standards (connect command policies to standards)
2) Contact with unit support agencies (both mission and community)
3) Calendar of social events (NCO)
4) Calendar of family events (Family Support Agenda)
5) Require NCO independent reading, study, and research

Diamond Point: If the former first sergeant has been coming into your "AO" too much in the last 30 days, run him/her off. Explain that you are in charge now.

6) Introduce five major changes in unit operations (many of these tasks should be taken from your implied tasks agenda)
7) Introduce your NCO-DP program (assign classes) (Develop or revamp based on need)
8) Create a Family Support Group/chain of concern (or add power to the existing group). Discuss social-psychological isolation among young enlisted family members.
9) Hold routine meetings with all junior enlisted soldiers. (Stress D.O.D. Reg 5500.7-R, Joint Ethics Regulation).
10) State that you will review the rough draft of all NCOERs required for submission the following month.
11) Publicize the NCO-DP stratification concept and use as a training tools to make the point.
12) Introduce a professional reading list for NCO-DP.

NOTE: *   Make a midnight visit to the unit.
       **   Back out now if you doubt that you are the best soldier for this job!

***   Ensure you again read the following:

1) AR 600-20   2) AR 600-200, Chapter 7, AR 608-99
3) AR 623-205   4) DOD Regulation 5500.7-R, Joint Ethics Regulation
5) AR 601-280   6) AR 600-9
7) AR 630-5   8) AR 600-31
9) AR 608-99   10) AR 27-10
11) AR 635-200   12) AR 614-200
13) 350 Series   14) System of checking DA Form 2166-8 of each platoon or section (SOP, LOI)
15) FM 22-5   16) AR 670-1
17) DA PAM 608-47, A Guide to Establishing Family Support Groups
18) AR 135-178, AR 140-10

3.   *D + 31 to D + 60:*

a.   Conduct a monthly NCO inductions ceremony (as required).

NOTE: The ceremony may be held at higher level of command.

b.   Introduce any other changes that need to be effected.
c.   Evaluate the acceptance of your methods of transitions.
d.   Hold your second meeting with all NCOs (CPL-SGM). (Stress D.O.D. Regulation 5500.7-R Joint Ethics Regulation)
e.   Establish your framework for leadership.
f.   Publicize all upcoming NCO events for the next 6 months (make known your attendance requirements).
g.   Announce the progress of the Family Support Groups (thank them for their interpersonal support). Show the connection of the FSG to the subjective combat effective indicator.
h.   Perform a health and welfare inspection on the barrack, auto, and work areas.
i.   Assess the relationship between officers and noncommissioned officers. Assess the pride in traditions and history of the unit.

    j.   Summarize your observations and assessments and brief the commander of your agenda.

    k.   Establish committees to plan and execute the unit's ethnic observances.

    l.   Provide your input to the Family Support Agenda (FSA).

    m. Schedule to discuss quarterly the topic—"Self-Sabotaging Tendencies

Diamond Point: Hold meetings when they are least disruptive to the unit's operations.

NOTE: Make a midnight visit to the unit.

    4.   *D + 61 to D + 90:*

   . . . make this quarter the "Squad Leader's quarter . . .

    a.   Summarize the progress of the Noncommissioned Officers. Revamp NCO-DP based on findings.

    b.   Assess the working relationship of the NCO and the officers.

    c.   Assess the officer's understanding of the NCO's duties.

    d.   Announce your recommendations of substandard NCOs for bar to reenlist (BTR). (Provide examples of substandard NCO's bullet comments).

    e.   Stimulate the Family Support Group (FSG) if needed by attending meetings.

    f.   Conduct your second NCO social function (informal).

    g.   Conduct monthly NCO induction ceremony (as required).

    h.   Assess the unit's ability to communicate with itself.

    i.   Review the Family Support Agenda (FSA) with the NCOs (DA PAM 608-47).

NOTE: Make a midnight visit to the unit.

    5.   *D + 91 to D + 180:*

   . . . remain aware of what is going on in the internal world . . .

    a.   Assess your unit's NCO-DP and revamp it when necessary.

    b. Inform NCOs on the "state of the unit" as you assess it. Include both the subjective and objective combat effectiveness indicators.

    c. Counsel those NCOs you identified for BTRs. Submit packets or allow a new period for reassessment.

    d. Perform a health and welfare inspection of work areas, autos, and barracks.

    e. Announce the unit's overall progress by publicizing what is and what is not working well.

    f. Conduct your third NCO social function (formal).

    g. Conduct a monthly NCO induction ceremony (as required).

    h. Meet with the ethnic observance committee (EOC). [See the Command Sergeant Major for Ethnic Observance L.O.I.]

    i. Assess the quality of the unit's training meetings.

    j. Present a class on D.O.D. Regulation 5500.7-R, Joint Ethics Regulation

NOTE: Make several weekend visits to the unit.

6.   *D + 181 to D + 365:*

. . . praise the accomplishment of platoon sergeants this period . . .

    a. Fine-tune all established programs.

    b. Eliminate anything that serves no need for mission accomplishment or for the soldiers.

    c. Refocus on new programs as they develop.

    d. Eliminate anything that inhibits or restricts total duty performance of any soldier(s).

    e. Provide quality feedback concerning the unit's training strategies developed to rectify training deficiencies.

    f. Recognize those NCOs who have been instruments of leadership.

    g. Conduct your fourth NCO social function (informal).

    h. Conduct monthly NCO induction ceremony (as required).

    i. Submit additional BTR on NCOs or remove those BTRs that have served their purposes.

    j.   Publicize all upcoming NCO events for the next six months.

7.   *D + 365 to D + 545:*
("Seasoned" if you make it to this point.)

    a.   Have an NCO social function (informal) to mark your NCO team one-year mark of progress. It is important to acknowledge teamwork.
    b.   Use the first 30-days of this period to reexamine programs and progress.
    c.   Look at your first year's milestone chart; continue to use those items that enhanced the command climate.

8.   *D + 545 to D + 730*
(Reinforcement and Sustainment):
Diamond Point: An informal social function could be something as simple as "chips and dip" in the dayroom or as complex as meeting at an eating establishment.

Diamond Point: Conclude that this has been the best two years of your life.

First Sergeant's Chronological Milestone Chart
Post-Position Period (PPP)

Post-Position Period:

1.   Apply these commandments of Post-Position:

    a.   Don't look back.
    b.   Don't make any attempts to effect any changes that you did not complete while in the position.
    c.   Make as few visits to your former work site as you need to, at least until the new guy gets established. Understand that you are seen as a threat.
    d.   Correct unit personnel when they refer to you as first sergeant.

e. Offer advice to the new guy only if he or she asks for it; only if the new first sergeant is a close friend is it proper for you to offer advice.

f. Explain to the commander, who may remain upon your departure, that he or she has a new first sergeant now and the above apply, then move out.

g. Spend as much quality time with your family as you can.

h. Your deliberate consideration of your future activities is most important.

i. If you realize that there is some command information concerning personnel, mission, or equipment that must be passed on, pass that information through the CSM to the new first sergeant.

Diamond Point: You must give the new first sergeant all the breathing room that you can. The worst thing you could do is sit around the orderly room talking about the way you did it or the way you would do it if you were still the first sergeant.

j. If the new diamond wearer calls you for some information concerning the company's equipment, personnel, or mission, give him or her just the information requested. Do not continue the conversation with comments about what you would have done if you were still there.

Diamond Point #1: This is one of the professional codes to allow the new guy breathing room.

Diamond Point #2: This is one of the codes of the professional to support the new guy on the block.

Diamond Point #3: The way I prevented anyone from claiming that I said something that I did not say was a simple matter; I made it known that I would confront those people and ask for a repeat. I also made it quite clear in all my professional dealings, that if something needed to be said, I would say it.

k. About two months before you terminate, begin to make a list of things you want to pass on to the new first sergeant concerning mission, personnel, or equipment.

Diamond Point: If you care about your Army and your soldiers, make the transition for the new guy a good one. Provide as much information as needed, then become scarce.

Two Techniques:

Two techniques that essentially supersede all other are negative digression mode and the positive progression mode.

Negative Digression Mode (Siege Mentality):

. . . time lost getting ready . . .
The negative digression mode is so called because while you are trying to get your feet on the ground, negative things that have been happening continue to happen. The first sergeant can recover from the effects of this mode, but not without a substantial loss of time. Once assigned to a unit, time is of the essence depending on the unit's profiles.

Diamond Point: When you are in charge, you are in charge of time, as well as space and people.

Presented here are some examples of the negative digression mode that you should not fall victim to.

1. You wonder openly if you can make changes to the charge-of-quarter instruction book after realizing that it is substandard.
2. You are not able to present the commander and the NCOs your plan of action within the first few days (implied tasks agenda).
3. You sit in your office more than 95% of the day for the first two weeks.
4. You ask the commander whether you can rearrange the orderly room.
5. You watch all NCOs leave at close of business (COB) each day and do not question that.
6. You identify racial tension and elect to hide in your office.
7. You accept a high accident rate as the cost of the high levels of training.
8. You fail to seek the skills and knowledge of the command sergeant major.

9. You do not question the training information being provided for the command sergeant major's brief.
10. You fail to incorporate the senior enlisted to be involved in developing the junior NCOs.
11. You allow noncommissioned officers to present poorly thought-out training strategies.
12. You take no action to rectify the fact that the training meeting attendees have vague thoughts of long-range and short-range training plans.
13. You realize that training meetings are disorganized and everything but training is discussed, however, you offer no corrective action.
14. You noticed that for the third unit training meeting conducted that the command sergeant major is present, but you don't ask her to leave.
15. Two weeks have passed and not once has anyone said anything about the operation of a Family Support Group (FSG), you have inquired of the FSG's operation.
16. Violations of D.O.D. Regulation 5500.7-R, Joint Ethics Regulation are evident but you allow business as usual.

Positive Progression Mode:

... instantly effecting change

The positive progression mode is so called because, if you employe this mode at the outset, within a few days the soldiers will feel as if you have been there all the time. You will acknowledge to yourself that you are going through growing pains. However, the unit will never feel the negative effects of these pains, only the positive effects. For these and other reasons, the pre-position assumption period is critical. The pre-position assumption period gives you the capability to walk into the unit and instantly identify the good, the bad, and the ugly.

Presented here are some examples of the positive progression mode, and this is by no means all-inclusive.

Diamond Point: Make it a point to create your own list of the two modes. This practice will allow easy identification, so you can avoid the one and develop the other. Look closely at both the subjective and objective combat effectiveness indicators.

The correct mode (Positive Progression) is one of the following:

1. Based on how well you have prepared for this position, in the last few days you have observed two NCOs and reviewed their records, and your decision is to have BTRs prepared on both by morning.
2. All indications are that the senior leadership has not taken the interest in junior leadership that will make this unit excel, and you institute programs to correct the situation.
3. Many NCOs do not understand the intent of AR 635-200 as evident by the fact that in two days you have identified six soldiers for Chapter 13 or 14 action and one soldier for Chapter 15 action.
4. Observing the wear of the uniforms and noting the many violations by NCOs, you designate certain Chapters of AR 670-1 as the subject of your first NCO-DP classes.

Diamond Point: Ask yourself this question for your own development: Are the soldiers violating the regulation because they do not know or do not care, or are standards known but not enforced?

5. Recognizing that soldiers' honest grievances concerning their organizational life, duty time, educational opportunities, and the command climate are not accompanied by expeditious corrective action, you focus on the deficiencies.
6. Realizing that documents sensitive in nature such as NCOERs are not protected as required, you institute the corrective action using the "Personal In Nature" cover, secured areas, etc.
7. After reviewing several DA Forms 2166-8, NCOER before the form has been declared ready for AG submission, you lay down the standards IAW AR 623-205, and you make it clear that corrective actions can be painful.
8. You address the company leadership to outline your plan to prevent the officers from performing as squad leaders or platoon sergeants, laying down a well-defined sense of duty and responsibility.
9. You instantly correct the misconception that nonjudicial punishment will not be used when other non-punitive measures are more appropriate for minor infractions.
10. After observing several unit training meetings you completely revamp method and procedure to make the meetings more effective (able to provide the training strategies).

11. After evaluating the senior NCOs support of unit's Family Support Group (FSG), you direct greater participation and assign reading of the family support regulation(s).
12. Constantly find ways to interact with the unit members.

Diamond Point: As you observe, monitor, evaluate, institute, direct, correct, alter, instruct or in some other way affect procedures, you establish your NCO Development Program.

13. Finding no evidence of ethnic observance, you identify and establish committees to plan and execute command ethnic observances.

... focus on anything that is broken ...

These two modes can also very easily be identified in your subordinates and will have similar affects on them. With your understanding of these modes, the wisdom will allow you another lever in one-upmanship as the leader. This duty of first sergeant is a very serious position. You touch the lives of too many of America's finest to do a "half-assed" job.

Diamond Point: All of the above is no more than exhibiting the ability to process information and perform multiple, complex missions and personnel tasks.

Readiness:

... focus on molding squad members ...

The way you sustain warfighting readiness goes beyond molding unit missions into a manageable group of training tasks. Molding that mission without molding the very nucleus of the unit, which is the squad member, is like building walls before laying the foundation. First sergeants do not directly mold squad members; that is done by the subordinate leaders below the first sergeant. However, the first sergeant task (FSST) that focuses on sustaining warfighting readiness is to ensure that the subordinate leaders are molding the squad member to support warfighting readiness.

... molding the molder ...

First sergeants ensure properly molded squad members by ensuring properly molded platoon sergeants and squad leaders for warfighting. Who trains the platoon sergeants and ensures he or she trains the squad leader? Separate the tasks in that question. One is to train platoon sergeants and the second is to ensure the platoon sergeants train the squad leaders. If the first sergeant fails to understand this very important point, the unit will never complete the warfighting molding process. The better the unit completes the warfighting molding process, the more proficiently it accomplishes the mission. The second and most important point is to ensure that all subordinate leaders understand factors of the warfighting molding process. Some of these factors are procrastination, loyalty, the hardness of war, team building, trust, turbulence, honest errors, and the rites of passage.

Diamond Point #1: Stress the uniqueness of your unit to your soldiers that they are the best at what they do.

Diamond Point #2: Promote the "Warrior Spirit."
    The warfighting molding process essential element is trained enlisted leaders who understand the full extent of their doing tasks (DTs), direct supervising and supporting tasks (DSSTs), and the follow-on supervising and support tasks (FSSTs). It is only in this understanding that training will be elevated to the command's training standards.

EXAMPLE

Doing Task (DTs)	Direct Supervising and Supporting Tasks (DSSTs)	Follow-On Supervising and Support Tasks (FSSTs)
Prepare rough draft training schedule for next training meeting.	Discuss with the platoon sergeants their input to the training schedule.	Observe soldier's performing training task and make note of quality as well as poor performance.
	Trouble with the platoon sergeants conflict of events time, equipment, etc.	Spot check equipment for readiness

The diamond is the master sergeant's best friend.

First sergeant, if asked to provide the
psychological profile of your unit
(soldiers and family members),
what would be your answer(s)?

First sergeants psychologically touches
the soldiers' being in such dynamic ways that the
effects are part of the soldier until death.

"That diamond worn by the first sergeant belongs to every soldier (enlisted
and officer) in the unit."

CHAPTER II

CONNECTION

◊   An Introduction

◊   Corps Interaction

◊   To Sign Or Not To Sign

◊   Types Of Duties

◊   Duty Interlock

◊   Service School Requirement

INTRODUCTION

The first Diamond Point of many in this chapter is that you, the diamond wearer, must be ever mindful of your relationship with the person you will be working for, however long it may be. You should concentrate on making it quite clear to your boss that you are not his or her servant, but the top supporter of his or her efforts to be successful. Those are the code words—to be successful.

The second Diamond Point that you must make to your boss is that he or she must talk to you about anything and everything. When and if you find that you have a boss who can talk to everybody but you, then understand that your team has not gotten past stage one. There are many, many reasons you two must talk, but the chief reason is that talking will help you get to know one another. Despite the fact that one of you are commissioned and the other is not, you must be able to look each other square in the eyes and say—that was dumb. Now you do understand that it must be done at the right time and the right place. If you know each other, hard feelings will not develop if your boss tells you you've done something stupid. You will realize that someone you respect is giving you advice that you should pay attention to. Open communication will also clear the way for positive actions in your unit.

Team Standards:

The team must establish a certain period to talk about the soldiers, the mission, personal things, and concerns. do not be hesitant to talk about anything important that will develop this relationship. When all is going well, talk about your life as a child, talk about the things that bother you in this life and talk about where you want to go with your life.

However brief this connection in your life may be for the two of you, it will be of significant value to you both for the rest of your military lives. Sad as it may be, many of these connections die the day of the change of command. However, some connections end only at the grave side. The point here is that while you are in effect a command team, it must be an effective command team, one that all other commanders and first sergeants within the command envy. Your command working relationship must be one worthy of modeling.

Negative Molding:

Now a Diamond Point that I do not like to address but must because of its importance is taking good notes. "To be successful" are the code words you live by. There will be those who allow you every opportunity to meet that goal. There will be those who will assume that you are useless to their success, and there will be those who, if allowed, will only use you and others to make them successful. Then there are those who will allow themselves to be influenced by everyone but you. Those who do not allow you every opportunity to help make them successful will necessitate good note-taking on your part. In addition to keeping good notes, you need to raise matters of concern to the command sergeant major. There is no one more aware than I that this situation crosses the borders of loyalty. A piece of advice—don't classify these matters as "officer business" or "NCO business," it is all Army business. If you know of a violation and do not stop or report it—you become part of that violation. Loyalty must be within the frame of ethical value.

Diamond Point: Keeping good notes will help you to produce that smoking gun.

Connection:

Corps Interaction . . .

The relationship between the commander and the first sergeant is a connection that causes the interaction between the Officers' Corps and the NCO Corps. This relationship implies that a command team's chief concern should be the enlisted soldiers of the organization.

In most cases, the commander will not have the luxury of selecting the top enlisted soldier. Therefore, he or she will not get the chance to match personalities. Each can make the other successful, or one can cause the other to fail. The commander and the first sergeant must be able to communicate their visions to one another and then to the command. Even if given the opportunity to select, there are not guarantees that the two will match.

So, first sergeant, the commander spends two weeks checking you out and reviewing what you have or have not done. You should give that commander a run for the money by presenting your visions in action. If you have nothing to show then you have a problem. This is one of the few times that you really need to ring the enlisted bells. Show the commander that the days of the "dumb sergeants" are gone.

A first sergeant should never give up his or her values and loyalty to the soldiers who he or she represents. It won't matter what good things you have done if you have violated your values in support of a command action that was not in the best interest of the soldier. This command team that you are a part of has to maintain balance in its internal structure. Keep in mind that you both share the results when one of the team members goes astray of the mission goals.

You and the command team must maintain open communication so that you can say, "You might not want to hear this boss—but you were wrong." When you cannot tell the commander what you think, then the "time out" flag must go up. Commanders, as well as first sergeants, are made of "human stuff."

To Sign Or Not To Sign . . .

In one of your initial meetings with the commander, you should determine which items that you as first sergeant, will be allowed to sign for the commander.

In all that you do, the soldier's requests or requirements for action should be the center of all personnel action. Routine matters, even though normally signed by the commander, should not be delayed because the commander cannot be found to sign the action. An action is important when it is important to the soldier. To sign or not to sign—that is the question. Some of the generalized legal actions that you should never sign are:

◊1.◊v Matters involving soldiers—civilian-connected, income-producing activities.

- ◊ Matters of debt counseling (critical stage).
- ◊ Matters of real estate, mortgages, complex wills and testaments, leases, or deeds of trust.
- ◊ Legal matters with civilian law involvement.
- ◊ Adoption.
- ◊ Citizenship and naturalization.
- ◊ Matters involving the validity of a contract.
- ◊ Divorce or separation proceedings.
- ◊ Board actions or court-martial proceedings.
- ◊ Matters concerning private property damage.

◊   Soldier claims against a private establishment.
◊   Chapter actions.
◊   Bar-to-Re-enlistment (BTR).
◊   Matters involving medical discharges.

Note: Discuss with the commander when you are not sure.

Routine Matters . . .

Routine matters, such as signing a form that allows a soldier to go to an office for some personnel action does not require the signature of the commander. You must examine the document before signing to ensure that it is correct and complete.

Establish a list of documents and forms the commander wants you to sign, and take notes on how documents should be checked before signing.

If you feel that the commander should be made aware of certain documents or forms signed in his or her absence, inform the commander upon his or her return.

Diamond Point: The routine world should not stop when the commander is gone.

Types of Duties . . .

First sergeant, before you can psychologically or in any other mental way forge this relationship, you should have a complete understanding of the three types of duties: specified, directed, and implied. You must know how these three duties are related to your boss. Failure to initially grasp the relationship of these duties with your boss' duties will only make the growing pains worse. As time passes and you become seasoned, you will easily be able to see the connection of duties.

. . . specified . . .

The commander's specified duties are not your specified duties because the regulation so states that the commander would, will, should, may, or could execute or not execute certain actions. Within those specified duties, there is no mention of the fact that the commander has a helper who is just as responsible for these specified duties. However, even though you are not specifically charged with these duties, your position gives you an important part to play. That role makes your position all the more significant.

Learn all you can from Department of Defense or Department of the Army publications concerning those duties that are specifically addressed to the commander. These publications will clarify issues that you and the commander will be confronted with on a daily basis. Do not wait until you are confronted with an issue to begin study.

... directed ...

The commander also will be given directed duties, verbally or in writing, that are not necessarily spelled out in regulations or manuals by his or her boss. Even though the orders were given to the commander, because of your position, you have a part in carrying out these duties as well.

... implied ...

Implied duties are the leader's people-oriented, catch-all duties that are not spelled out in military publications or verbalized. The real source of the power of this duty is experience and knowledge-honed and sharpened by years of development and study. Implied duties have more of a universal application than the other two types of duties.

Unlike those duties specifically stated in a Department of the Army or Department of Defense publication (specified duties), and unlike those duties that are requirements and may be given verbally (directed duties), implied duties carry a very distinct characteristic—the amount of individual soldier's control over these fundamental duties that are essential to the day-to-day effectiveness of the U.S. Army. These unwritten duties support the other duties. Your ability to create and maintain cohesive teams depends on how well the implied duties are executed.

Another differentiating factor is that the implied duty of exerting influence will increase as the rank increases, whereas specified duties decrease as rank increases. The military system includes an unwritten understanding that as you advance in the grades, so should your knowledge and understanding of the requirements of the implied duties.

Diamond Point: While studying the commander's duties, translate them into your implied duty box.

Duty Interlock ...

The interlocking of the commander's duties (specified) and the first sergeant's (implied) duties determines how well this leadership team will function. An industrious diamond wearer will know the commander tasks that contribute to any one specified duty. The first sergeant pays even more attention to those tasks of the commander that fall into the glass-ball category than those that fall into the rubber-ball category. In the event the commander has to go on an emergency leave, or on TDY, the diamond wearer will be able to ensure that the commander's replacement stays on track and keeps certain important actions moving.

A newly appointed diamond wearer who does not immediately understand the above facts is oftentimes put into uncomfortable predicaments because he or she is not able to act or react to the commander's specified duty problems. That is another reason the newly appointed first sergeant needs to establish strong relationships with other diamond wearers and draw from their experience in putting those frameworks in place. Do not be an island unto yourself.

Because there are so many specified duties charged to the commander, factors such as the command, the mission, and the assigned personnel, will have an effect in determining which specified duties are most important.

Diamond Point: Some of the commander's specified duties are more important than others. You should make a habit of writing down those duties determined to be most important.

Service School Requirements . . .

The service schools' course curriculum should therefore focus not only on the specified, directed, and implied duties of the diamond wearer but on interlocking with the commander's specified duties as well. Both positions must understand the interrelationship of their duties upon the assumption of their duties, and not a year into the tour. Once that simple fact is understood, then the diamond wearer can concentrate on transforming the commander's specified duty into an implied diamond wearer's duty. The diamond wearer would then be able to find any commander's specified duty in the appropriate publication and break that specified duty down into tasks supporting the diamond wearer's implied duties.

The NCOs who have held this position have learned to do that, but they have not understood the technical aspects of this transformation of duties. In other words, we have been doing it all along, but we could not explain it until now. by adding this to the schools' curriculum, the process would become an integral part of the first sergeant's support role to the commander. The better our Army understands this process the more success stories can be attributed to this important command team. First sergeants are not born, they are made.

Diamond Point: A really good commander will ensure that his or her first sergeant knows what the important commander specified duties are.

Every most qualified soldier with a sequence number is not meant to be a first sergeant, I don't care how much the battalion commander likes him or her.

Don't allow procrastination to drain you of creative energy and rob you of the one quality that matters most in leadership: the feeling of being in charge.

CHAPTER III

INTERACTOR STAGE 3

◊ Steps to the Top

◊ Religion

◊ The Supportive Spouse

◊ Commander

◊ Command Sergeant Major

◊ Platoon Sergeants

◊ The Spirit of the Unit

The fact that Reserve Components Units
participate in numerous overseas deployment
for training exercises equates to a requirement and
institutionalized Family Support Groups.

Step To The Top:

Keep yourself ready to assume the duties and responsibilities of the leader(s) at the next higher level. (Learn the specified and implied duties at the higher level.)

Ladder of Success—Groundwork for Competence

+----------------------------------+-------------------------------

Ensure a well-rounded military education
(Conduct independent reading, study, research)

+----------------------------------+-------------------------------

Analyze yourself objectively
(Strengthen the strong, overcome the weak)

+----------------------------------+-------------------------------

Cultivate a genuine interest in people
(Understand capabilities and limitations)

+----------------------------------+-------------------------------

Develop a philosophy of life and work
(Support your self-analysis)

+----------------------------------+-------------------------------

Foster association with success
(Study and observe it)

+----------------------------------+-------------------------------

Diversify leadership assignments and positions
(Strengthen the experience factor)

+----------------------------------+-------------------------------

Admit mistakes and accept criticism
(In these two elements are growth)

+----------------------------------+-------------------------------

Master uncontrolled emotions or negative habits
(Indicate a lack of leader self-control or leader discipline)

+----------------------------------+-------------------------------

Optimistic outlook
(Seek opportunity to win by capitalizing)

+----------------------------------+-------------------------------

Pass these lessons learned on to your subordinate leaders
(Your greatest legacy)

Stage Three:

Interactor Stage #3 is no more than asking the questions,
"How did I get here?" and "How do I now share the wisdom of my success with others?" At this stage, you say to yourself, "I have broken the codes of Interactor Stage 1 (squad leader level) and Interactor Stage 2 (platoon sergeant level). How do I now pass the baton (lessons learned) back to my subordinate leaders?" It is not how much you know that makes you a success, but how much your subordinates know as a result of your teaching that makes you a success.

Implied Duty . . .

◊   nourish the morale of your unit
◊   cultivate the art of delegating responsibility
◊   maintain your integrity to enhance growth
◊   apply common sense to ensure success
◊   give rewards and punishments according to merits
◊   share hardships and dangers
◊   demand courtesy
◊   encourage initiative in soldiers
◊   keep abreast of command policies
◊   in the face of popular disagreement, stand for what is right
◊   do not allow NCOs to abdicate their duties and responsibilities at will
◊   share professional reading list

Religion:

First Sergeant, there are elements in your command/community that are important, and that you should become involved in. Religion is one of those important supporting elements that we often overlook. I could go into a long spiel about religions and beliefs, but my objective is to point out the important part you play in religion within the command.

Your attendance at church services will have a tremendous affect on the command. You will be surprised at the number of people who will start going to church because you go. They will be there mainly because you are there. Do not be against anything that is positive for the command.

In your prayers to this God, who you may or may not believe in, tell Him that your attendance is your contribution. What the command gets out of the service, in the spiritual sense, then or in the future, is not the chief concern to you as a leader. They are in the service because you are. You will have helped some lost sheep back into the fold: maybe, just maybe, something will transform them while they are there. And maybe when you leave the command, they will continue to attend the worship services.

Be aware of the affects you have on more than military life. Be a forerunner in any aspect of the community that you can. Influence is a very powerful tool that builds the command.

Diamond Point: Keep in mind that religion means different things to different soldiers. Ensure soldiers respect other soldiers' rights to be different.

—The Supportive Spouse—

Note: Please read the book, The First Sergeant Spouse Notes

Introduction:

... maintaining a balance ...

The spouse in the military (SIM) is responsible for the attainment of numerous leader goals and objectives for a successful military career. There are certain fundamental facts that will help you, the spouse of the SIM, to break the code. You need to be somewhat of a psychologist and have a clear, valid understanding of your military spouse and of his or her motivations, attitudes, aspirations, and the increasingly complex military system. These fundamental understandings are required in order to maintain the best possible balance between military life and family life.

... is a multiplier ...

The military spouses (MS) who breaks the adjustment code first and foremost must understand that the demands of military life go far beyond those of their civilian counterparts and greatly contributes to their understanding of how to be a multiplier. She or he then whole-heartedly supports the achievement of the spouse in the military (SIM), having broken the "Code." Military life will pull on those binding ties and test their strength, you can count on that.

Prerequisites:

The prerequisites to becoming a successful military spouse can be established through a series of questions that you, the military spouse (MS), should seek and demand answers for. These are only a few of the questions that require constant analysis by the military spouses (MS):

Supportive Spouse Questions:

1. What is the military and what are the requirements of its members? How do those requirements affect me and us as a family?
2. What are some of the military terms that I must learn to further my understanding of military life?
3. What are my spouse's motivating factors, aspirations, values, and attitudes?
4. How can I enrich my life to enrich the life of my spouse in the military (SIM)?
5. How can I keep my spouse in the military looking and feeling good about what he or she does?
6. What are the "Principles of Military Spousehood?" (See "Steps to the Top.")
7. What does my spouse in the military know that I must learn to ensure that those elements are reinforced?
8. What exactly are Army Regulations and their intent?
9. How can I help organize and promote a program of learning?
10. What are the Army Publications that I must have a working knowledge of to help my spouse in the military?
11. What classes are available to teach the spouse about the military?
12. What community activities do I want to be involved in or have time for?
13. How many hours a week can I devote to support or attend military or community functions/activities (See the D.V.O. Model: ZERO to FIFTEEN).

Support Positive Behavior

... complementing and reinforcing ...

Your understanding of your spouse's (SIM) behavior will help you acquire the ability to influence his or her behavior by complementing and reinforcing his or her goals. There are factors that cause your spouse in the military to take certain actions that are important to success. Learn what they are! Stay attuned to his or her emotional, physical, and mental stability.

The spouse in the military (SIM) has esteem needs that stem from the desire for appreciation, recognition, and respect.

... supporting esteem needs ...

Any time the SIM receives a promotion, decoration or an award of any kind, small as it may be, express your appreciation and feelings in some tangible way that supports this esteem need. You satisfy this need in part by ensuring that your commitment and expectations are in line with your spouse in the military. Small as these awards seem now, they are part of the building blocks to the top.

Spouse Vocabulary

... learning the military language ...

A vocabulary of military terms is a must for the purpose of communicating with your spouse in the military (SIM) and being able to fulfill the role of an effective supporter. In addition to observing her or his every action, you should learn from the following terms, and have a serious discussion with your spouse in the military (SIM) about them:

- Cheerless hospital rooms	- Family Support Group (FSG)
- Discipline	- Proficiency
- Family Advocacy	- Sponsorship
- Esprit-de-corps	- Professional Development
- The Phantom's Philosophy	- Ethnic Observance
- Morale	- Aggression
- Proficiency	- Frustration
- Leadership	- Rationalization
- Motivation	- Basic Allowance for Quarters

- Tact	- Basic Allowance for Subsistence
- Article 15	- Variable Housing Allowance
- Loyalty	- Active Component (AC)
- Integrity	- Organizational Life
- Authorization	- Family Support Agenda (FSA)

Diamond Point: Depending on your spouse's other organization family members, she or he will need to understand the military language.

Spouse Vocabulary

Abbreviations . . .

- ARTEP, Army Training and Evaluation Program
- AT, Annual Training
- C2, Command and Control
- C3, Command, Control and Communications
- CG, Commanding General
- CP, Command Post
- CTT, Common Task Training
- EDRE, Emergency Deployment Readiness Exercise
- ETS, Expiration Term of Service
- 1SG, First Sergeant
- FTX, Field Training Exercise
- LBE, Load Bearing Equipment
- LOI, Letter of Instruction
- METL, Mission Essential Task List
- MOPP, Mission-Oriented Protective Posture
- MOS, Military Occupational Specialty
- NCO-ES, Noncommissioned Officer Education System
- OJT, On-The-Job Training
- PCS, Permanent Change of Station
- SPC, Specialist
- ALICE, All Purpose Lightweight Individual Carrying Equipment

* Incomplete List: See also Chapter VII and the book, The First Sergeant's Spouse Notes

... establishing your own list ...

There are more words to add to your vocabulary. Have your spouse add to this list. It will take you time to learn, and to be able to apply these terms correctly. My wife's military introduction was a slow one and she still has trouble with the ranks, however, she was always the one who stuck with me for study through the midnight hour when the platoon sergeant had to go home to his own family. She did not completely understand the questions or the answers, but she was there.

The Supportive Spouse (leadership multiplier) ...

... very much attuned ...

It should be called breaking the "Code." Many a spouse breaks the "Code" the very first day the spouse in the military (SIM) begins to wear the symbols of leadership. These quality people, the military spouses, are as much attuned to the traits and principles of military leadership as their other halves (the spouses in the military).

"Proverbs"

Who can find a virtuous spouse? For her (his) price is far above rubies.

The heart of her (his) spouse doth safely trust, so that she (he) shall have no need of spoil.

She (he) will do him (her) good and not evil all the days of his (her) life.

She (he) seeketh wool, flak, and worketh willingly; with her (his) hands.

He (she) riseth also while it is yet night, and giveth meat to his (her) household, and a portion to his (her) maidens.

She (he) openeth her (his) mouth with wisdom.

She (he) looketh well to the ways of her (his) household, and eateth not the bread of idleness.

Her (his) children arise up, and call her (his) blessed; her (his) spouse also, and she (he) praiseth him (her).

Family Support

She (he) wants him (her) to be a contributing member of this great Army. The home environment must then be one where all family members strive to assist the soldier in attaining the intermediate goals and objectives. The Family Support Group provides the soldier with assurance that the army takes care of the family.

. . . recognizing your support . . .

Your military professional (SIM) has undergone special preparation and training, but often, too often, the one support system that contributes most to that preparation is the supportive spouse, and we (the military) often, too often, forget to recognize that support. The most common qualities of this leadership multiplier are being attuned to the personalities and qualities of successful leadership; being involved in not only the development of a program of learning but also the programs of sustainment as well; being aware of the effects of the home environment on the professional; being willing to use what has been learned to provide much needed external support to the younger professional military spouse—a genuine care for people.

His or Her Place

. . . pride and dignity of the professional . . .

The military spouse knows that the military professional provides a living, however, the military spouse also shares that certain pride and dignity of the professional. To the military spouse, professionalism will be intangible, difficult to describe, and hard to measure.

. . . successful personality traits . . .

Your military professional must learn to identify the traits of successful leaders, such as bearing, courage, dependability, endurance, enthusiasm, integrity, initiative, and loyalty, to name a few. Some of these traits will be discussed in detail later because they can be applied to you as well.

Inspector/Evaluator

. . . how to become the quality controller . . .

The military spouse (MS) must become an inspector of the military professional each time he or she prepares to perform, ensuring that sharpness that only an extra set of eyes can ensure. The spouse in the military learns that the Army is a uniformed service where discipline is judged, in part, by the manner in which the military professional wears the uniform as prescribed. You may wonder how to become the inspector (quality controller). There are Army regulations or publications that cover everything you or your spouse want to know. Therefore, to serve as quality controller, ensuring that conditions of clothing and equipment are exemplary, read the regulation that prescribes the authorization for wear, composition, and classification of uniforms, as well as occasions for wear. This publication also will tell you the accouterments, insignia and awards authorized for wear, and how these items will be worn on the uniform (AR 670-1).

Spouse Human Behavior

. . . when adjustments are needed . . .

Observing certain human behaviors that would indicate whether adjustments need to be made, such as your spouse's level of confidence, level of alertness, and level of energy, is nothing less than what you would do for the family car.

If profanity is a part of your professional's speech, keep telling him or her that it indicates a lack of self-discipline and self-control. Soldiers always have resented being sworn at by their leaders. Profane or obscene language causes friction, resentment, and even insubordination. Practice removing these words from his or her vocabulary by having your soldier write down these words on a slip of paper and bring them to you for disposal. As with any other bad habit, you must work to break it.

Bearing

. . . setting the example . . .

"Bearing" means control of one's actions and emotions and implies a state of being honorable. Soldiers lose respect for leaders who make spectacles of themselves through loudness, needless expressions of anger, immoderate language, and alcohol or drug abuse.

The bottom line is that you should help the professional concentrate on achieving and maintaining the highest standards in conduct and appearance. Bearing is setting the example.

Courage

... willingness to assume and share hardship ...

You also must understand the importance of courage, an essential element that will allow your spouse in the military to concentrate on maintaining, achieving, and proceeding with firmness and calmness in the face of criticism or danger. Courage is a mental quality, therefore, it will be difficult for you to gauge this quality in your spouse. However, by understanding this mental quality, you will be able to help resolve some of the frustration associated with courage.

Your spouse's fortitude is essential if he or she is to stand up for what is right for the subordinate in the face of unpopular agreement or popular disagreement. Actions are commendable that demonstrate your military professional's willingness to assume and share hardship and danger with the soldiers.

Your Program of Learning

... the honest evaluation ...

Talk to your spouse in the military (SIM) about military publications and which section or article could help you with your task as the honest evaluator. Once you are shown the materials to read, prepare notes and questions to review with your spouse. Create study guides from the material you read and continue to develop these guides as you are given additional information. When your spouse in the military least expects it, pull out the study guide and drill your spouse in the military. These drilling sessions will aid you in your learning too.

Proficiency

... knowing what has to be done and how to do it ...

Why is your involvement so critical to your spouse's proficiency? The answer is simple. If your military spouse is deficient in carrying out her or his responsibilities, then the contemporaries, superiors, and most important, the soldiers in your spouse's charge will lose confidence in his or her effectiveness to accomplish the mission. This loss of confidence should be prevented at all costs, for this is what your spouse in the military is all about-accomplishing a mission.

COMMAND SERGEANT MAJOR (RET) BOBBY OWENS

Subject Matter

... helping to develop ...
What are some of the subject matters that should be included in your framework for spouse learning? What should every soldier know? What combat-operation elements should be known? Ask what administrative and technical knowledge must be stressed? Most importantly, ask what general subject areas are useful, such as:

- Uniform (wear and appearance)
- Weapons (general information)
- Map Reading
- Counseling
- Guardianship

- NBC
- Marksmanship
- Physical Training
- NCOER
- Family Care Plan

Why? If the military spouse has a well-rounded general overview of the subjects then they can better understand what is being said.

Supporting Self-Improvement

... leadership is not easy ...
... supporting leadership is not easy ...
The honest evaluation that you will have to give will not be an easy task to perform. These evaluations, however, will help your spouse in the military (SIM) determine weaknesses and strengths that will result in a better soldier once the limitations and capabilities are known. Get your SIM to trust you as an honest critic. Find out from your SIM what would further develop strengths and eliminate weaknesses.

... sharing philosophy ...
You must ask your spouse in the military to share with you his or her philosophy of military life and work. If you do not write them down while they are being given, then do so later. These philosophies are important to development.

... honest interest ...
Think, while reviewing these philosophies, what part you will play. Your part is to support the non-military efforts and understand the reason for his or her military actions or behavior.

You, as the military spouse, can help arm your spouse in the military with your honest evaluations in order to support the sound tactical and technical background required to perform military duties.

Proficiency: Yours . . .

. . . do not be turned off . . .

Military publications and the jargon therein may turn you off; it sometimes turns off the soldiers for whom it is written. However, dull as it may be, this is the source from which your spouse will extract the knowledge that will make him or her proficient. Have your spouse in the military walk you through AR 670-1.

. . . respect and confidence are not automatic . . .

Keep in mind that your spouse in the military will not automatically gain respect and confidence from his or her superiors, contemporaries, or soldiers because of position or rank. Support your spouse's study and independent reading for a well-rounded military education.

You can help your spouse in the military be a good example for his or her soldiers by encouraging constant training, study and proper planning.

Right Time To Talk

. . . times for peace of mind . . .

I always stressed to my beloved spouse that I could fight the external world all day long, but when I came home I initially wanted peace of mind. She understood that, and waited for better opportunities to discuss some of the less desirable issues of the day. She learned the best time to confront me. She would start by saying, "Is this a good time to talk about your family?" This would always cause us both to laugh. Or, she would tell me something that she had heard that was funny. Once we had had our laugh, then I knew that the funnier the joke, the weightier the matter was that she had to discuss. There is a right time and a wrong time. The two of you must work out that best time.

"Leadership is not easy—it never was meant to be."

The Author

Supporting Military/Community Functions and Activities

You, the military spouse, should be the one who decides how much time you will dedicate to military or community functions. Please ensure that your reasons for contributing your time include a genuine interest in people.

The community needs strong advocates for the concerns of enlisted soldiers and their families. The junior enlisted spouse does not realize the number of confrontations that will be endured or the amount of personal time that will be given.

My wife devised the "Zero to Fifteen" plan, which aided her in determining just how much of her time she could allocate per week. Your choices range from "0," doing nothing, to unlimited service. The D.V.O. Model is a suggested starting point. You will be able to add to this list or even rearrange this model to fit your schedule.

Leadership
... It includes setting tough, but achievable standards and demanding that they be met; caring deeply and sincerely for subordinates and their families and welcoming the opportunity to serve them; ...

AR 623-205 • 15 MAY 2002

ZERO TO FIFTEEN—(D.V.O. MODEL)[1]

1-2 HOURS

* Call Junior Enlisted Spouses just to see how they are doing

* Send out welcome notes to the newly arrived spouse

* Send out notes of congratulations to those whose spouses were promoted or were award recipients

STOP

* Attending only Company Change of Command Ceremonies

* Attending only Bn level Change of commander

* Provide input into the Family Support Agenda (FSA)

NOT MORE THAN FOUR HOURS

* Include the 1-2 hour's list

* Visit selected junior enlisted spouses for friendly conversation

* Visit newly arrived spouses to the command to welcome them

* Meet with other first sergeant spouses to discuss some command family issues

* Attend all Bn level or lower changes of command ceremonies

STOP

* Attending all Memorial Services with my spouse

* Attending meetings with FSG leaders and unit representatives

* Help to publish the Family Support Newsletter

* Submit input to the Family Support Agenda (FSA)

NOT MORE THAN 6 HOURS

* Include all 1-4 hours' list

* Attend meetings for the following organizations only:

STOP

* Attending all Family Support Group meetings

---

[1] Family support model used by Dorothy V. Owens, the wife of a first sergeant to help manage her time as a first sergeant's wife.

-Commissary Council
-Post Exchange Council

NOT MORE THAN 8 HOURS   *STOP*
* Attend all Change of Command Ceremonies

* Attend all Community Quality of Life Seminars

* Attend all meetings for the following organizations:

-Commissary Council
-NCO Club Council
-Installation Improvement Council

* Include all 1-6 hours' list

* Round out time with hospital visit (family members)

NOT MORE THAN 10 HOURS   *STOP*
* Include all 1-8 hours' list

* Attend all meetings for the following organizations:

-Commissary Council
-NCO Club Council
-Installation Improvement Council
-Education Advisory Council
-Post Exchange Council

* Once a month, visit with the organization's commander

* Participate in Officer's Club spouses' interaction

NOT MORE THAN 15 HOURS   *STOP*
* Include all 1-10 hours' list

* Meet with the Sponsorship Welcome Committee

* Work with FSG leaders and unit reps to prepare next FSG newsletter

*   Check the operational readiness of the FSG and FSG Volunteer Roster by calling those listed. (There are other ways of checking the Operational Readiness of the FSG)

NOTE: This model is only one example of a time management tool.

CHAPTER IV

ACTION

◊ Center Focus   Part I
◊ Relief for Cause   Part II
◊ Monitor   Part III
◊ Framework For Leadership   Part IV

- Sponsorship
- NCOER System Review
- Company Operational Systems
- Developer (of future leaders)
- Promotion Advice
- NCODP
- Junior Leaders
- AWOLS
- Creator
- Updating

Actions: Part I

Center Focus . . .

Many duties to be performed by the first sergeant are unparalleled by any other leader's duties in this military occupation. However, four top actions must remain the center focus of the first sergeant duties. The four actions are: (1) to stand between the officers and all enlisted soldiers, (2) to ensure that all NCOs are engaged in a systematic effort to acquire a body of knowledge appropriate for his or her role as an NCO, as well as his or her military occupational specialty (MOS), (3) to dedicate oneself to the welfare of all your soldiers and their families, and (4) to ensure that training is not action conducted to appease the higher-ups.

I have always maintained that every officer is not meant to be a commander, and every sergeant is not meant to be a first sergeant. Understanding the officers' socioeconomic background compared to the enlisted soldiers' background is an important key in understanding this focal element. What is important to officers may not be important to the enlisted. Cultural and educational levels will cause the two groups to always look at things differently.

Officers historically have been placed on a pedestal. The officer corps no longer requires money or property to raise and equip the Army. However, the "mightier than thou" remains a blight of the officer corps.

Officer soldiers are different from enlisted soldiers, and their elevated status should not be changed. What should be changed is any thought process that does not support the fact that the American enlisted soldier is the most noble of creatures on God's green Earth. Any thought process contrary than that should attract your artillery fire.

No leadership doctrine, written or unwritten, maintains that one is the slave of another. No law says that because of position, one will be allowed to treat another in any way desired. The principles of military leadership apply. The traits of leadership apply. Violations will be dealt with, or you will have allowed one of the most sacred of your duties to be desecrated.

Diamond Point: There will be symptoms before you realize the sickness.

Officer's Program of Learning:

Senior NCOs have no idea what junior officers are taught in the Army's institutional systems of learning. The problem then becomes determining what ongoing information the NCO corps offers that improves upon of what the junior officer *has* already learned? The Army transfer/transition can be conducted with much more structure if the institutional stop point was known. This is another system failure that we acknowledge and must correct. If the NCO corps knew more about the common subjects portion of the institutional program of learning for officers, then the NCOs could better teach the junior officer the "ropes."

Unanswered Questions:

What are officers told about NCOs? What are officers told about junior soldiers? How are the junior officers told to interact with the members of their first units? What are junior officers told concerning their relationship with the unit's first sergeant? Where do the NCOs go to determine the answers to these questions?

Research conducted on the officer corps has not extended into the program of instruction for officers' courses. However, *The Armed Forces Officer* (1975 edition), American Forces Information Service Department of Defense, was most informative. Chapter 20, Relationships With Your People, outlined very well some of the elements that contribute to a solid command climate. This chapter points out lessons that should be part of the programs of learning in our military learning institutions, at all officers' and NCOs' basic and advanced course levels.

Numerated below are the points from Chapter 20 that would greatly aid officers' and NCOs' development:

1. An officer should never speak ironically, or sarcastically, to an enlisted member, since the latter doesn't have a fair chance to answer back. The use of profanity and epithets comes under the same heading.

2. Upon meeting an enlisted member of his own unit in a public place, the officer who does not greet that person personally and warmly, in addition to observing the formal courtesies between people in service, has sacrificed a main chance to win

the individual's abiding esteem. If it is a man with his family, a little extra graciousness will go a long way, and even if it didn't, it would be the right thing.

3. In any informal dealing by an officer with a group from his own unit, it is good judgment to pay a little additional attention to the youngest or greenest member of the group instead of permitting him to be shaded by older and more experienced members.

4. It should go without saying that an officer does not customarily drink with his enlisted people, though if he is a guest at an organizational party where punch or liquor is being served, it would be a boorish act from him to decline a glass simply because of this prescription.

5. Visiting unit members in a hospital is a duty that no officer should neglect. Not only does it please the person and members of his family, but it also is one of the few wide-open portals to enhance loyalty.

6. . . . If the officer has reason to think that the treatment being given falls short of the best possible, it is within his or her charge to raise the question.

7. A birthday is a big day in anyone's life. So is a wedding, or the birth of a child. By checking the roster and records, and by keeping an ear to the ground for news of what is happening in the unit, an officer can follow these events.

8. Nothing is more pleasing or ingratiating to any junior than to be asked by a superior for an opinion on any matter, provided it is given respectful hearing.

9. . . . It is the task of the officer to see that all is right, and to take the trouble necessary to make certain of it. If the officer is doubtful about the mess, a mere picky sampling of the food will do no good. Either he will live with it for a few meals, or he won't find the "bugs" in it.

10. . . . Orders hesitatingly given are doubtfully received.

11. An officer is not expected to appear all-wise to those who serve under him. Bluffing one's way through a question when ignorant of the answer is foolhardy business. "I'm sorry, but I don't know," is just as appropriate from an officer's lips as from any other. And it helps more than a little to add, "but I'll find out."

12. Rank should be used to serve one's subordinates. It should never be flaunted or used to get the upper hand of a subordinate in any situation save where the latter has already discredited himself in a unusually ugly or unseemly manner.

13. When a subordinate has made a mistake, but not from any lack of good will, it is common sense to take the rap for him rather than make him suffer doubly for his error.

14. An officer should not issue orders that he cannot enforce. He should be as good as his word, at all times and in any circumstance.

15. An officer should not work looking over his people's shoulders, checking on every detail of what they are doing, and calling them to account at every step. This prissy attitude corrodes confidence and destroys initiative.

16. The identity of the officer as a lady or gentleman should persist in relations with people of all degrees. In the routine of daily direction and disposition and even in moments of exhortation, the officer had best bring courtesy to firmness. The finest officers are not occasional ladies or gentlemen, but in every circumstance—in commissioned company, and, more importantly, in contact with those who have no defense against arrogance—exhibit courteous behavior.

17. As with any other introduction, an officer meeting an enlisted man for the first time is not privileged to be inquisitive about his private affairs.

18. . . . So long as a subordinate is just a number, or a face, to the officer, there cannot be a deep trust between them. Anyone loves to hear the sound of his own name and when his superior doesn't know it, he feels like a cipher.

19. . . . Man is of flesh and blood and will fail in crisis if he has been pushed too far. But in the military, he is also a member of a great brotherhood whose fellowship can make the worst misery tolerable and afford him undreamed strength and courage.

20. . . . These are among the things that need to be studied and understood. It is only when an officer can stand and say that he is first of all a student of human material that all of the technical and material aspects of military operations begin to conform toward each other and to blend into an orderly pattern . . .

Action:

Transition Interaction Integration . . .

Transition Interaction Integration (TII) is the process through which a new member of an organization/unit must go in becoming a part of the spirit of that element. A certain percentage of officers will have trouble with the process, while others will have smooth TIIs. Some have trouble with the process for many reasons, from fear to differences in socioeconomic backgrounds. The fear concerns being newly confronted with interaction, while being pulled in different directions.

Diamond Point: The best time to get a good mental feel for a new officer is upon the new officer's entry. You can have a large impact on an officer's TII by what you do and say those first few days. If you are a member of one of the advance thinking units, in which it is a requirement for you, the diamond wearer, to talk to all newly assigned officers, you will be able to set a progressive tone for interaction. In many of the units I grew up in, the diamond wearer wanted to show newly assigned officers how powerful they were and ignored the newly assigned for months. The new school of thought maintains that complete team interaction needs to begin as soon as possible. Ensure he or she understands your charter and relationship with the rest of the unit and that you represent the enlisted soldier's interest first and foremost. Talk about your frameworks of learning and leadership.

. . . stressing interaction . . .

Stress at the onset the importance of officer and enlisted interaction as well as the limits of interaction. Discuss how you, with the officer's feedback, can help him or her be successful. Also stress the development program with officers and NCOs.

Breaking the socioeconomic barriers will not be as easy as dealing with that newly introduced environment. Buried deep within the minds and hearts of some newly assigned officers are undefined and unjust perceptions of minority soldiers. Some of them will not have had to interact with a minority until assigned to your unit. Their assignment will require you to become a social worker.

Diamond Point: I always told those who were having problems with this portion of TI to think of peace and war. If the unit were ordered into combat today, could or would you feel safe to turn your back to your own soldiers? We never know the hour at which the call will come. War is very much like death. We know not the hour it will come. Create in peace that which we can, with confidence, go to war.

The Courage: The trait of courage, which requires us to tell an officer that his or her actions are not in keeping with the spirit of the chain of command, is on the agenda during your tenure as first sergeant. This action, as with any action, requires the use of tact.

... the human touch issue ...

The officer who experiences little or no pain in TII is well on his or her way to becoming part of an effective team. The focus then must be on officers who have trouble acquiring and applying the human touch. First sergeant, keep your eyes and ears open and attuned to the activities of the unit. Soldiers will report it to you when it happens. The spirit of the unit also will indicate the need for your attention. When that need presents itself, reach out and touch someone for the record. The worst thing you can do is to pretend the need is not there.

A memorandum of record for future reference is a tool you should always employ.

Diamond Point: Transition Interaction Integration (TII) is a special segment of the unit's reception and integration process.

Diamond Point: All of the following have to be addressed when processing transition interaction integration:

- diversified American culture   - organizational life
- ethnic observance   - command climate
- bi-cultural family programs   - self-sabotaging
     tendencies

Of Human Stuff ...

Yes, we can say that in contrast to European countries, Americans traditionally have never sought to draw their officers from a particular class. We have drawn thousands of commissions from the battlefield in the past four large wars, and they were the proud and the humble, as well as the rich and the poor . . . However, we are not in total agreement with Voltaire's words, "Whoever serves his country well has no need of ancestors."

Take notes of these words from *The Armed Forces Officer* (1975 edition):

> Still we must deal candidly with the hard realities. The officer body, being of human stuff, is not without fault, folly, and failing. Furthermore, the public affection, while hardly fickle, is not so constant that there need be no concern about rewinning it through merit and greater dedication to duty (page 2).

Diamond Point: This is by no means an attempt on the part of the author to debase the officer corps, however, there will be officers who do not believe that the officer's body is of "human stuff" and without fault.

Diamond Point: The first sergeant stands to the four sides of the unit analyzing the function of the "human stuff" of all leadership groups. The diamond wearer promotes the force that combine the soldier power of these diversified groups and directs it toward the common objective.

The Philosopher-Leader . . .

Plato maintained that the people will be properly governed only when the wisest men, the philosophers, are given power.

> " . . . there will be no end to the troubles of states, or indeed, . . . of humanity itself, till philosophers become kings in this world, or till those we now call kings and rulers really and truly become philosophers . . . There is no other road to happiness, either for society or the individual."
>
> *Plato*

. . . what is the focus? . . .

Philosopher-leaders would not be interested in money, power, NCOER, OER, etc. They would not act out of ignorance or prejudice. They would only be interested in candor, commitment, courage, and competence. These philosopher-leaders would spend many years getting the education and experience needed to become leaders. They would only be the wisest and best of soldiers, the only ones fit to lead. These leaders would insist on respect of truth, moral education, and deep commitment to ideas.

... leader's agenda ...

Philosopher-leaders continuously validate their commitment to that which he or she professes to be committed. These leaders keep foremost in mind that where they are removed several levels higher, they should never forget what it was like at lower levels. The organizational life of the soldier is always one of the top priorities on these leaders' agendas in their discussions of the quality of life in the barracks. They remember their days there.

Diamond Point: Teach them the interpersonal skills as a part of all that is done.

Understanding Officers ...
(The Armed Forces Officer, 1975 edition)

Among the precepts, or gentle qualities, desired in military officers of the U.S. Army are these:

1. Dedication to human rights.
2. Respect for the dignity of the individual.
3. Fair play to all and favoritism toward none.
4. An active concern for all aspects of human welfare.
5. The will to deal with every person as considerately as if he were a blood relative.

Only the strong can hold to those principles. But there is no more certain measure of a person's capability to pursue a single-mindedly a high purpose despite all temptation (page 4).

-   On becoming an officer, the individual should not renounce any part of his or her fundamental character as an American citizen. He or she has simply signed on for the postgraduate course where one learns how to exercise authority in accordance with the spirit of liberty. The nature of his trusteeship has been subtly expressed by an American Admiral: "The American philosophy places the individual above the

84

state. It distrusts personal power and coercion. It denies the existence of indispensable men. It asserts the supremacy of principle" (page 5).
- We beget goodwill in others by giving it. We develop courage we show in our own actions. These two qualities of mind and heart are the essence of sound officership. One is of little avail without the other, and each helps to sustain the other. As to which is the stronger force in its impact upon other people, no truth is more certain than the words written by the psychologist and philosopher, William James: "Evident though the shortcomings of a man may be, if he is ready to give up his life for a cause, we forgive him everything. However inferior he may be to ourselves in other respects, if we cling to life while he throws it away like a flower, we bow to his superiority" (page 3).

First sergeant, you should not have to protect the enlisted soldiers from officers, but it is indeed sometimes necessary. Identifying when you need to build a heat shield between the enlisted corps and the officer corps will require experience.

... pre-training process aids interaction ...
The ways in which officers interact with the enlisted depend on many forces that are too numerous to list. However, the pre-training process (both at home and in society) and the officers' social economic background are factors. Your duty is to be ever mindful that all soldiers are not inducted with the right military ideas and some soldiers are never transformed to the military way of thinking. If you are aware of such activities that are not in keeping with either the "Spirit of the Chain of Command" or the "Spirit of Freedom" and you do not take action to stop it—you then are a part of the problem. You should simply, either bring the matter to the attention of a higher authority when it is not stopped by the local authority or turn the entire case over to the Inspector General (IG).

... using internal assets ...
Draw on the knowledge that which the officers bring to a unit when teaching new or little-learned skills. An English major can do wonders in an NCODP program in which one of the objectives is to improve writing skills.

Diamond Point: Solicit all officers in the area, not just those assigned, to help you improve knowledge of your soldiers.

Diamond Point: The first sergeant broadcast continuously the fact that the American soldier is the noblest of creatures on the face of the Earth.
Diamond Point: The diamond wearer does not allow situations that deteriorate teamwork or does not support positive socialization.

Action:

NCOs . . .

The Egyptians faced life with confidence, felt that their pyramids and temples would last forever, and that man could do all the great things in this lifetime that he wanted to. In contrast, the Mesopotamians thought man was no more than a slave of the gods, that man was unimportant; therefore, Mesopotamians felt helpless and afraid in life.

. . . instilling confidence . . .

As different are the attitudes between the Egyptians and the Mesopotamians, so are the attitudes among the members of the NCO Corps. Some are helpless and afraid. They are not sure what should be done, what could be done, or whether they possess the necessary authority. They are caught up in a tremendous series of merry-go-rounds, unable to control their own direction. Such a condition first sergeant, is a serious deficiency in our corps that must be corrected.

As leaders confronting this serious deficiency, you should simply take action as with any problem-solving situation. If you allow this deficiency to thrive, then you are counter-productive to our goals and objectives. NCOs who share the life view of the Mesopotamians rather than the Egyptians, must be taught the dynamics of the Corps. Most important of all, NCOs who maintain the Egyptians' "can do" attitude should not allow those with the Mesopotamian's mentality to set the standards.

The next step is to ensure the NCOs know what bars-to-reenlistment are and how BTRs can effect their lives.

The following are examples of the serious deficiencies a first sergeant should target:

◊   Failure of the NCO Corps members to become serious students of the external as well as internal systems that affect their soldiers.

◊ Conditions that violate the personal professional pride of the NCO Corps.

◊ Conditions that discourage initiative or limit latitude, or that restrict total duty performance of NCOs.

The Mesopotamians were able to find excuses for their condition in life, to escape life's realities. You should not allow the Corps to digress to these conditions of yesteryear.

NCOs' Progressive Development . . .

An NCO Corp member is non-productive who struggles alone day to day and is not engaged in learning about the systems (personnel, maintenance, supply, training, safety); the human element (soldiers and families, superiors, peers, and that external world of the human element); the NCO him or herself (an objective evaluation); and how these elements fit together.

. . . assuming the knowledge of NCOs . . .

Never should you assume that NCOs know what they should know in order to function and to do their jobs well. It is not their fault either that they don't know as much as you want them to, it is most often the fault of the systems. However, the one element who can correct this shortfall in the systems is the first sergeant. NCOs are caught up in the day-to-day mission and they won't have time for the degree of development that the system should be requiring. The future will require nothing less than a fully developed NCO. As a result of the mission requirements, the burden of self-development will fall heavily on the individual.

. . . affecting soldiers attitudes . . .

All too often, the attitude the soldier develops is based on the attitude emanated by the NCO. This point that should be considered carefully in our teaching of the Corps in setting the example. Even in the worst situations, the leader is able to hold the team together with his or her attitude. How does an attitude hold a team together? This question must be answered by each leader. No book can explain how the leader's attitude holds the team together. The first sergeant, however, should have the answers to aid the confused leader who struggles with the question.

Group vs. Team:

If and when a platoon loses confidence in its leader because of his or her attitude, the leader no longer has an effective team that is capable of carrying out its mission. The platoon becomes a group of people who will accomplish something, but not the mission that is the goal, and not in the desired manner. They are an ineffective team.

An ineffective team is looked down upon as "dud." It is not because the internal operating core (the soldiers) is dud, it is because the platoon leadership is uninspired. The leader lacks the proper attitude that supports team building and team motivation. Consider this a deplorable state that requires your attention. The Army does not need another ineffective team. Those who look down upon this element and declare them to be "dud", should also behold the element's rise from "dud" status. This will be a lesson to others who follow in your footsteps.

Tolerating ineffectiveness . . .

If you tolerate an ineffective team while you are a member of the command team, allowing a leader to deny his or her soldiers their followership rights of effective leadership, then you, my friend, become a part of the problem and demonstrate ineffectiveness in carrying out your duties. An unseasoned platoon sergeant is a leadership challenge that must be added to your already full plate. The longer you allow this negative command element to exist the more difficult it will be for you to turn the situation around. By tolerating ineffectiveness, you violate your framework for leadership. Military professionalism cannot abide ineffective platoon sergeants or ineffective first sergeants who allow ineffective platoon sergeants. You should have methods to identify and eradicate ineffectiveness.

It is a matter of principal to keep the commander informed of your development objectives. The commander who resents your efforts is a moderate or low achiever and you must learn to adjust to that situation.

How should you react to these dysfunctional organizational situations (DOS)? Harassment of a soldier by an officer is initially somewhat like sexual harassment, and should be dealt with, somewhat like sexual harassment. Just tell the officer that soldiers are not to be harassed but taken care of. Inform the harasser that a memorandum will be written describing the conversation and will be given to the CSM.

Next, use the chain of command and write a memorandum describing your conversations about the situation. In the event that the situation cannot be initially corrected, the memorandum then becomes an invaluable tool in building a credible case to present to the chain of command.

Diamond Point: You must understand what dysfunctional organizational situations (DOS) are. The answer is very simple. Anything that prevents or decreases the quality of effectiveness of mission accomplishment and the welfare of the soldier is dysfunctional.

Diamond Point: The unit's leadership groups are under an informal contract to assure soldiers their followship rights of effective leadership.

Dedicate oneself . . .

First sergeant positions have their own peculiar rewards. Chief among them is the opportunity to become acquainted with the nation's finest and the nation's worst. Then, therefore, dedicate yourself. If you have always maintained that the noblest entity on God's green Earth is the American soldier, you will perform your job well. Do not take the job if you cannot completely dedicate yourself to the position.

Your Word . . .

When your team learns to trust what you say, they will develop an attitude that fosters unit proficiency and individual productivity. The strength of the unit, and the well-being of all your soldiers depend upon your constant reaffirmation of the trustworthiness and virtue of "the position".

Diamond Point: The diamond wearer is trained to engulf the psychological being of every soldier in the unit.

Diamond Point: The diamond wearer also must continuously develop that sixth-sense that enables the wearer to detect soldiers who demonstrate less than their full potential.

Diamond Point: The first sergeant's performs the direct supervising and supporting tasks (DSST) and follow-on supervising and support tasks (FSSTs) by incorporating every member of the leadership groups into the development process.

Action: Part II

Relief for Cause . . .

This portion of The Diamond opens with a barrage of thought-provoking questions aimed at preventing this most devastation career stopper. The questions we need to ponder collectively are.

1. What is the relief for cause?
2. Who initiates the relief for cause?
3. Why is the relief for cause significant in a soldier's military life?
4. Why would a relief for cause be initiated by anyone other than the rater?
5. How is a relief for cause identified?
6. What should happen to the soldier after receiving a relief for cause?

What is the relief for cause?

The relief for cause is an action that must be taken by members of the chain of command when there are gross violations of standards or conduct, or failure to keep within the spirit of the chain of command. Relief is defined as the removal of anything painful or burdensome by which some ease is obtained; ease from pain, grief. Quite the contrary, the relief for cause is one of the most painful actions an NCO can undergo during his or her career, whatever the cause. The soldier is taken out of positions of leadership (authority and/or responsibility).

We further define relief for cause as the removal of a soldier from a rateable assignment based on a decision by a member of the soldier's chain of command or supervisory chain when his or her personal or professional characteristics, conduct, behavior, or performance of duty warrant removal in the best interest of the U.S. Army (AR 600-20, para 3-13-Relief for Cause).

Involved . . .

Very few negative personnel actions will have the same effect on a soldier as the relief for cause action. Regardless of rank or position, no soldier deserves to be jerked around because of someone's gut feelings. In the cases involving enlisted soldiers in your unit, get involved, whether the relief is justifiable or not. Get deeply involved.

Command Influence . . .

Your involvement should first of all include a thorough review of the case, the competency of personnel handling the case, and the amount of command influence in the case. Your involvement is to ensure justice is done to and for the accused soldier. Once you are satisfied in your mind that the system is working to maintain justice, that is as far as you should intrude into the matter. Do not allow yourself to be accused of trying to insert command influence. Whenever you question anyone regarding a case, state that the questions are for clarification only.

Once the results are in and the case is in its final stage, again look at all the evidence as an outside observer. If you are required to make recommendations, then do so in the interest of justice. Never allow the command to become embroiled in an influence situation because of your actions.

Relief for cause is an ignominious necessity that we must support. However, because it is so dishonorable and shameful, you must take care to ensure the actions described in the next two paragraphs are in keeping with the chain of command.

Advice . . .

Relief for cause should never be a moot action, after the fact. In the cases that can be anticipated, the leader affecting the relief should seek your judicious advice before the hatchet falls. Your years of service have given you the ability to develop a perspicacity about significant emotional events. The leader effecting the relief should confer with you to alleviate some of the inherent insidiousness of the action.

Requirement for Professional Counseling . . .

Relief for cause actions can be so emotionally devastating that the affected soldier or the soldier's family members may require professional counseling. You must be aware of this fact, and the command should be instigating this action. The affected soldier will in most cases demonstrate resiliency that belies their feelings of persecution.

Future Reference . . .

A memorandum of the relief should be written for future reference describing the events of the relief for cause action. Include a description of your involvement and whether you provide counseling for the soldier who received the relief for cause.

Diamond Point: A first sergeant going through a period of trying to determine what duties and responsibilities the position entails, is putting in jeopardy the well being of all the soldiers in the unit.

Action:

Monitor: Part III

◊ Sponsorship
◊ NCOER System Review
◊ Company Operational Systems
◊ Developer (of future leaders)
◊ Promotion Advice
◊ NCODP
◊ Junior Leaders
◊ AWOLS
◊ Creator
◊ Updating

Leadership is intangible,
hard to measure,
and difficult to describe.

Monitor: Part III

Sponsorship . . .

(See Annex A)

The special instruction for sponsorship duties (see Annex A) ensure that the sponsor understands *not only his or her duties but the importance of the program as well.* These instructions are direction for the sponsor after the incoming soldier has arrived.

We cannot expect or assume that our soldiers know what to do when they are assigned a duty. The bad taste that starts in the incoming soldier's mouth that first day could stay with him or her for the entire tour of duty. Furthermore, if called upon to perform the duties of sponsor, the soldier will perform them as he or she saw them performed.

Once you establish standards for sponsorship, monitor the program, evaluate the program, and enforce the standards set. This is a leadership requirement that, when delegated, is still managed at the top. The NCOs of the organization must have the same vision of sponsorship. They are the ones who will enforce this standard. Sponsorship is your responsibility. Sponsorship involves building morale of your command members as they walk through the door. The payback is too great to leave this important standard-setting task to subordinate leaders.

Diamond Point: Reception and integration is an implied leadership function that every leadership group must be involved.
Diamond Point: Every leader must read DAPam 608-47 and enjest the concept of the Family Support Group (FSG).

Monitor:

NCOER System Review, AR 623-205 . . .

First sergeant, with your knowledge of the importance of the NCOER concerns to NCOs and their families, you cannot allow substandard rating officials to produce adverse reports without adhering to the system guidelines. If substandard rating officials lose sight of the evaluation system's objective, then you must bring them back to reality.

You must ensure the rating officials understand that the NCOER is designated to strengthen the ability of the NCO Corps to meet the professional challenges of the future through the inclusion of Army values and basic NCO responsibilities; and to ensure the selection of the best-qualified NCOs to serve in positions of increasing responsibility by providing rating chain views of performance/potential for use in centralized selection, assignment and formation of Enlisted Personnel Management Systems (EPMS) decisions.

The following are the first points to review in ensuring officials' actions are in keeping with the spirit of the chain of command:

1. Monitor the rating officials to determine whether they are developing a genuine interest in the soldiers they rate. Indicators to the contrary are failure of the officials to read the NCOER regulation, failure to develop a knowledge and understanding of the rated soldier, or failure to give timely counseling to the rated soldier.

2. Determine how active the rater is in recommending or helping the rated soldier seek a well-rounded military education by supplementing attendance at a service school with independent reading, research, and study. Monitor in particular an official of a rated soldier who can neither write or speak well. The rating official should help the rated soldier by requiring that he or she go to the education center.

3. Determine whether the rating officials are using all reasonable means to become familiar with the rated NCO's performance throughout the rating period. Some rating officials will make such a claim, but will not have time to counsel the soldier when required.

Diamond Point: The scope of the counseling is only limited by the rater's knowledge of the soldier and the system.

4. Ensure that fair, correct report evaluations of the NCO's duty performance, professionalism, and potential are prepared by the rating officials.

5. Ensure that performance standards are communicated to the rated soldier.

6. Develop a knowledge and understanding of your subordinate.

7. Notify the commander of any rating official who is deficient in carrying out official duties.

8. Analyze the mutual respect and confidence between the rating officials and the rated NCO.

9. Determine whether rating officials are allowing their soldiers to develop their own techniques for performing tasks.
10. Ensure that the spirit of initiative in the rating officials' subordinates is promoted.

Diamond Point: Define for all the term "rating official." Everyone must take seriously the duties of an official.

Diamond Notes
(concerning the NCOER system)

Diamond Point: "Rating Official" must have a good understanding of the basic understanding of human behavior which is a prerequisite to being an effective rating official.

Diamond Point: The diamond wearer does not permit members of the unit where morale, discipline, proficiency and esprit-de-corps are held in the highest to maintain the title of rating official without taking on the follow-on implied tasks.

Monitor:

Operational Systems . . .

Do not ignore seemingly minor problems in your unit or feel that they will go away. Why do you need an outside agency to tell you what you already know is wrong? Why should you have to live in a constant state of apprehension as to when the dam will break?

Evaluating the System

Constantly evaluate your operational systems that support missions or soldiers and determine what needs to be fixed and how. Take the system apart to see what needs to be replaced. Spare not one facet of the operation from critical review!

Diamond Point: Keep in mind that you need always to be harder on yourself than anyone else could possibly be.

In evaluating the complete operational systems, understand that you are not the expert in all areas. The secret is to have your operational personnel give you a brief and for you to know enough about the operation to ask the right questions. Any questions that cannot be answered by operational personnel during the brief should be answered as soon as possible. Teach the personnel to know more about the subject of their specialization than anyone else. Teach your operational personnel to back up what they say with a military publication.

Diamond Point: You must learn to become a scrutineer (one who scrutinizes).

Diamond Point: The most effective leadership is a network of many small thing, all of which converge to bring the participants into the alternative reality of the leader.

Diamond Point: Another first sergeant teaching point is to note the established connection of the leadership group's emphasis regarding the unit's NCOER processing.

Diamond Point: The first sergeant then compares the quality of incoming soldiers with bullet comments of the D.A. Form 2166-8.

Diamond Point: There should be some form of tangible evidence that the rater has shown interest by observation and shown standard improvement requirements.

Action:

Developer (of future leaders) . . .

◊ Promotion Advice
◊ Junior Leaders
◊ AWOLS
◊ Creator
◊ Updating

> "The most efficient first sergeant will fail
> if he or she is the only person in the unit
> who understands the operational aspects
> of the first sergeant's position."

Promotion Advice . . .

The name of the game is not how good you think you look to a promotion board, but rather how you compare with those of equal rank in your career management field (CMF). The problem here is that you will never know how you compare with other soldiers in your CMF. The comparison is made by the selection board; you are compared to the standard and then to your peers'. The soldier can only focus on the standards, and not on his or her peers progress.

How can you help soldiers understand that what the selection board sees is what they evaluate for promotion? Those of you who have been successful and understand the system that promotes excellence must now identify those NCOs who need attention. Understand the system and develop early the structure that will be in place at review time. No one is ever "ready for the board." It is ridiculous for an NCO who is months from the primary zone to express urgency in meeting requirements that will require time. The records I reviewed on the DA selection board indicated too many cases of last-minute efforts that failed.

View the Records . . .

The Department of Army selection boards that I sat on made me happy that I was a self-motivated soldier. When we discussed records of soldiers who had fallen short of promotion, if we concluded that the soldier did not care, at that point we could not care. We realized that it was too late to help those soldiers advance. You, diamond wearer, must insist that supervisors take care of their soldiers by allowing them time to attend school, forcing them to take courses, and counseling them on their military future beyond the next grade. The success of those of lesser rank is a burden the leader must bear.

I was not convinced as I graded records that the NCOs were aware of the importance of their records' appearance. Considering the level of records I reviewed, I as a senior NCO was disappointed in the condition of the records of Air/Land Battle Army leaders.

Diamond Point: All diamond wearers must understand that the NCO must develop in the whole soldier concept. Senior soldiers have to grow across the board, engaging in tactical learning/technical learning and civilian education/military education because they will develop their subordinates the same way that they as senior leaders develop.

NCOs are grown by senior leaders. Assessing the development of one's military life is a serious task that is too often overlooked. The diamond wearer must be mindful of not only his or her own career, but also of the careers of each soldier entrusted to his or her care. Overseeing careers is really developing the Army of Air/Land Battle. An important footnote to that is that minds engaged in career development are not in trouble. Soldiers will feel good about themselves and will want great things for the unit. They will not always appreciate being forced to further their education. However, in the future they will thank you for what you helped them do today.

The opportunity to develop is no longer the subject of NCOs dreams. The system has laid the opportunity for education at their feet. The problem is that too many NCOs are stepping on or over that which is lying at their feet.

Diamond Point: The first sergeant's follow-on supervising and support tasks (FSSTs) demands that the first sergeant be an active participant in every soldier's career development.
Diamond Point: Include career developmental activities in the unit's long-range planning.

Developer:

Junior Leader(s) . . .

The young officers as well as the NCOs, need your help for development. Many officers will not come to you or ask for your help in any way. Give them your help and advice freely and discretely. Discretion will ensure the increased efficiency of the command. If a young officer refuses to be advised on anything, a different course of action must be taken. For the most part, that officer will not admit ignorance of the concepts and procedures you have lived with for years.

Your commander (also being young) may have established other priorities that do not include structured learning of military concepts and procedures for the junior officers. The commander may even have missed a few of these concepts as he or she advanced. Therefore, you must offer a structured system of learning not only for your subordinates but also for those who might be looking in vain to the commander for that system of learning.

The very same subject matter presented to the junior NCO will be appropriate for the junior officers. The presentation does not have to be schoolhouse-style and volume does not matter. They need developmental information that teaches them where to find the answers to their questions at their present level. If you fail to aid the development of junior officers, nothing will be said. It is a task that is seldom mentioned on the NCOER.

Never pass up an opportunity by the commander to talk to the assembled junior officers. Subjects you should cover with the junior officers as well as junior NCOs are:

◊ Social-psychological relationships
◊ Officer and NCO relationships
◊ The importance of ethnic observance
◊ What all officer should know about NCOs' duties
◊ What all officer should know about AR 600-20 with regard to NCOs
◊ What all officers should know about AR 623-205
◊ What all officers should know about an effective NCOER
◊ What officers can do to enhance the academic status of NCOs
◊ Identifying combat effectiveness indicators
◊ Ways officers should affect morale of their soldiers
◊ What an enlisted soldier is and is not
◊ The role of officers and NCOs in Chapter Actions
◊ Promoting a spirit of initiative in subordinates
◊ Mastering an optimistic outlook
◊ Accepting honest errors with recrimination
◊ Capitalizing on a soldier's capabilities
◊ What is meant by the "silent cries for help"

Diamond Point: Study subject that will support the proficiency, morale, and discipline of the soldier.

Diamond Point: The first sergeant's doing tasks (DTs) provide the framework that keep the unit's junior leaders focused on the correct principles, concepts and doctrine.

Diamond Point: The diamond wearer's develop consistent mechanisms that will not allow the blurring of priorities that support improved proficiency.

Action:

AWOLS—The Prodigal . . .

Welcoming back the prodigals (sons or daughters) is a task that requires a human touch and a genuine feeling that the prodigal should be given the opportunity to start over, and he or she should make the best of this chance. If the prodigal is to be a productive member of the unit, further shattering that soldier's pride is counter-productive.

The manifestations of leadership qualities require the human touch. You should allow yourselves time to stop and focus on the fact that the prodigal is someone's son or daughter. Without making any excuses for the prodigal, I will say that any soldier who has been in the military for more than five years has had a reason to go AWOL because of poor leadership. The human touch requires that you put yourself in the soldier's shoes and ask the question, "What would I have done?" The human touch requires that you examine all the facts and judge the prodigal with an open mind.

Diamond Point #1: The deeper value of why soldier(s) go AWOL is to study the "why." Subordinate leaders need to retain lessons learned.
Diamond Point #2: Think! Do you think that the soldier should bear the brunt when poor leadership caused the soldier to go AWOL?
Diamond Point #3: As the first sergeant has learned, every leader must understand that the platform of exaltation is located on the road of humility.
Diamond Point #4: The evaluation of NCOs by persons not involved with their supervision is not authorized Chapter 2; AR 623-205
Diamond Point #5: . . . the moral principle that human beings should be treated with dignity and respect uplifts the human personality.
Diamond Point #6

Action:

Creator . . .

The first sergeant's position by design and authority position must be an astute creator of a healthy command. The command should include programs and systems that allow all the unit's soldiers to develop their full potential—systems of safety, suicide prevention, morale, esprit-de-corps, discipline, and training.

The first sergeant must establish and enforce regular habits of:

◊ Safety (in every aspect of the soldier's organizational life)
◊ Warrior spirit (ready for the war that is not hoped for)
◊ Maintenance (everything operational)
◊ Training (the hallmark of the soldier's daily activity) especially marksmanship
◊ Physical fitness (stress the connection to a sound mind)
◊ Professional development (a continuous process for all)
◊ Ethnic observance (stress the importance of every soldier)
◊ Support of family members <AR 623-205 • 15 May 2002>
◊ Sponsorship (reception and integration—the beginning of organizational life)
◊ Counseling (tell and show them how to improve)
◊ Assessment/evaluation
◊ Critique (with the purpose to improve all of the above)
◊ Family Support Agenda (FSA), DA PAM 608-47
◊ Ethics <D.O.D. Reg 5500.7-R, Joint Ethics Regulation>
◊ Identifying excellence (helps the soldier reach for new heights)
◊ Motivation

Soldiers by nature tend to keep the habits, good or bad, that they enjoy. Habits that require extensive effort will fall by the wayside when allowed to.

Diamond Point: Let outside agencies come in to help you with the above actions. Keep as many of these habits on the front burners as you can.
Diamond Point: All of the leadership groups must embrace these habits and not be allowed to pick and choose.
Diamond Point: The first sergeant's direct supervising and supporting tasks (DSSTs) requires that the diamond wearer include all of the above in the platoon sergeant's training program(s).

updating . . .

The command sergeant major (CSM) has a boss who he or she must keep informed by what he or she perceives and by what the first sergeant tell him or her. Commands above your level are, to say the least, somewhat removed from the human touch and the detailed, day-to-day operations. They have obligations that remove them from personal interaction level;

you must ensure that critical information flows upward. Information that would highlight the objective combat effectiveness indicators.

The CSM values the first sergeant who has good judgment in identifying what the battalion commander needs to know (whether critical or informational) and who passes that information along in a timely manner. The first sergeant does not overfeed the CSM with unimportant detail. The valued first sergeant selects the information that will prevent the CSM from getting broadsided. The CSM also values the first sergeant who provides follow-up information. The worse impression that a first sergeant can give is that he or she is an island unto himself or herself.

The CSM does not want or need to know everything going on in your unit. Internal personnel actions that involve NCOs are noteworthy. If the first sergeant feels that the matter will someday become the CSM's concern, then the CSM should be given a heads-up. The first sergeant should not wait until the eleventh hour to tell the CSM all of the problems he or she has had with an NCO.

Some of the information provided to the CSM may be sensitive or fall into an unreliable status. If so, make that known to the CSM. The CSM will then take responsibility for any premature releases of such information.

Diamond Point: Do not send your original or only copy of the memorandum for record (MFR) forward. Use your best judgment in choosing the method and personnel used to forward the MFR.
Diamond Point: Provide the CSM with written details of the unit's training strategies for the next training brief as they are developed.
Diamond Point: The diamond wearer supports the command sergeant major in systemic assessing and reassessing of these training strategies that keep the organization mission ready.

Actions:

* Frameworks for Leadership
  ◊ Section I—Introduction
  ◊ Section II—Frameworks—Failure As A Tool
  ◊ Section III—Continuous Process
  ◊ Section IV—Diamond Management Principles
  ◊ Section V—Diamond Caring Principles
  ◊ Section VI—Framework—Development
  ◊ Section VII—Framework—Evaluation

Section I: Introduction

Framework for Leadership . . .

Developing a personal and professional framework for leadership, not only for oneself but for the unit as well, will require energies even you did not know you had. At this point, you have been successful and now your mission refocuses on those soldiers you lead. Leadership, as you know it, is caring. Soldiers are your mission.

The framework for leadership is one that questions the status quo. You should be saying: I know that things can be better for my soldiers; I know that we can improve the organizational life; I know that we can train better; I know that the NCOs can progress mentally, thereby becoming greater assets to the command; I know that our soldiers deserve the best leadership; I know these things and will work toward their accomplishment.

As an infrastructure: The framework as we understand the framework to be, is the infrastructure that holds the outer structure up, much like the frame that holds the body upright, the skeleton. The leadership framework's backbone is as important as the body's backbone.

The framework for leadership demands that every NCO be actively involved in every aspect of the organizational life of all members. The stripes that NCOs wear take away the choice in becoming involved. When NCOs accept the stripes, they also accept the realities of the position, and many of the unit's NCOs will not understand that in this they have no choice. If the military system allowed soldiers to accept or reject at their whims, the result would be anarchy. NCOs who do not actively support matters of NCOs concerns, and who think they can choose their activities, should be on a collision course with you—the first sergeant. If you give them a choice in attending the dining-ins and dining-outs, most will not attend. With plenty of advance notice, these functions become duty.

Publicized: The framework for leadership cannot be some little idea conceived at midnight and carefully tucked away in the back chambers of your mind. That would be like tucking away a seed, waiting to be planted, away back in the dark barn. Your framework for leadership has to be an everyday part of your plan of action, well planned, well thought out, and well publicized. The results will be well supported.

The framework for leadership also includes the prompt recognition of honest grievances, prompt recognition of flaws in the soldier's organizational life, and detailed instruction on military discipline.

As you develop or create these frameworks for leadership, include all elements of its implementation and continuation. A framework that has the involvement of your subordinates stands a much greater chance not only of continuance in your absence or departure, but also of use by your subordinate leaders in their future endeavors. The development stage holds an NCODP lesson, that of developing these frameworks for leadership.

Diamond Point: Publicizing will ensure that your concept gets implanted into the minds of junior leader.

indicators . . .

The first sergeant's frameworks for leadership must include the specification that soldiers stand at parade rest when talking to a senior. Teach them why this is important with regard to discipline. When a soldier stands and goes to parade rest in the presence of a senior, it triggers one of the indicators of good leadership. Your framework for leadership is really an extension of your own military personality. All who come in contact with unit members will encounter that personality.

The frameworks for leadership postulate that leadership is not easy and it was never meant to be easy. The quest for another stripe should give leaders a desire to make everything better for the unit. The way to contribute to the Corps is to create methods of not only accomplishing the mission, but finding new ways of accomplishing the mission. Interject yourself deeply into the organizational life of your soldiers.

The Army is a uniformed service in which discipline is judged, in part, by the manner in which the individual wears the uniform. A vital ingredient of the Army's strength and military effectiveness is the pride and self-discipline that American soldiers bring to their service. (AR 670-1)

Translate . . .

Transferring your inner conviction about these frameworks to the unit subordinate leaders will not be an easy task. Your legacy in these frameworks is that they outline you in this position.

Diamond Point: Keep these frameworks for leadership on the front burners.

Frameworks for leadership also include:

. . . framework for training management
. . . framework of unit machinery maintenance
. . . framework for administration
. . . framework for marksmanship
. . . framework for human problems resolutions
. . . framework for counseling
. . . framework for ethnic observance
. . . framework for ethics
. . . framework for discipline and responsiveness
. . . framework for a basic understanding of human behavior
. . . framework for family support

The Frameworks for Leadership must complement and reinforce each other. The unit's leadership groups must understand the unit's programs in order to give maximum support for these frameworks. It does not matter how much you know, importance is given to what you know based upon what your leadership groups know. Impart that leadership knowledge to the unit's leadership groups at every opportunity. The framework for discipline and responsiveness supports the framework for administration because you would have systems in place to ensure that NCOERs were not late after receiving notification that the NCOERs were due.

Any requirement that involves the unit proficiency requires a framework for leadership.

Diamond Point #1: Examples of leadership groups are junior officers, senior NCOs, etc.
Diamond Point #2: Collecting known standards or creating and establishing new ones when required is the essence of developing the framework.
Diamond Point #3: Some frameworks require full SOPs or LOIs, however, most require only a page or so of explanation.

Action

Section II: Framework; Failure Training Tool failure allowed . . .

Development of these frameworks of leadership. is a conscious process to achieve a desired result. Keeping the unit motivated is your responsibility, first sergeant. Part of the framework in development is to be critical of your framework and make lessons out of failure. The trainer's failure must always be treated positively. Failure in training is part of development; the first sergeant must accept it and the unit's NCOs must accept it. But failures that NCOs do not capitalize on are true failures. Training failure is when training is not conducted in accordance with training plans, or when standards are not met or the soldier knows no more after the training than they did before the training. Training for success is just the opposite—the soldier knows more after the training than he or she did before the training.

Analyze what went wrong and don't sin by making the same mistake again. There will be times to put on your "ass-chewing" hat, but not at this point—wear your teaching hat. The first sergeant's teaching hat may require that he or she put on the subordinate leader's hat. A word of caution here: Do not put this hat on in front of the subordinate leader's soldiers. A training success results when the leader can openly admit a training failure and define the corrective actions. The worst failure occurs when the leader ignores the failure and goes on to the next training cycle or event.

In peace time, the first sergeant must allow training failure and build it (corrective action) into a training base. War-fighting proficiency is frequently built on mistakes and correction of training failures that test the leadership's stamina. The key focus is not just to correct training failures, but to prepare teams to operate independently of parent units while still performing missions following the overall intent of the commander.

Allowing and critiquing failures is how NCOs learn to act in a more critical situation where equipment could be destroyed or damaged, or even worse, lives lost.

Diamond Point: You, the senior leadership, make liars out of our junior leaders by not accepting some degree of failure.
Diamond Point: Training failure(s) require training strategy that support development. The diamond wearer never allow training failures to destroy a junior leader.

Section III: Continuous Process

The development of the frameworks of leadership. is a continuous process, requiring all subordinate leaders to understand that the task of leadership is never complete. If all the unit's subordinate leaders understand the forces and factors that produce the desired results, they will direct their efforts along productive lines. This concept supports the fact that unit proficiency is the sum of the soldiers' skills welded together by the leader into a smooth, functioning team. The first sergeant's frameworks of leadership. demand continuous high standards of group and individual performance. Only then will your unit attain high proficiency.

Diamond Point #1: The saying that is hard to paint a fast-moving train is very true. Once the frameworks are developed and published, they must never be allowed to be set aside by subordinate leaders because of mission requirements. The frameworks, by design, must be an integral part of the mission.

Diamond Point #2: The first sergeant should always encourage as well as reward recommendations for improvement of these frameworks and, where indicated, effect revision and refinement. Subordinate leaders will accept the frameworks of leadership better when their involvement results in improved leadership.

Diamond Notes: #3: The myriad list of activities that a first sergeant must accomplish is mind-staggering. The first sergeant's implied tasks agenda is a "well" without a bottom. Properly constructed frameworks of leadership. ensures that the first sergeant complete all doing tasks (DTs), direct supervising and supporting tasks (DSSTs), and follow-on supervising and support tasks (FSSTs) successfully.

Section IV: Diamond Management Principles

These are the principles that must guide the first sergeant and the unit's subordinate leaders. They all must understand the right ways of doing military business and how much latitude they have with their first sergeant. Herein are only a few of the suggested "Diamond Management Principles." The first sergeant have his or her own thoughts of doing military business. Most important is that the first sergeant publish these principles.

- Decisions on realignment of priorities should be directed to the necessary command level.
- These principles must be understood down to the lowest level. The first sergeant directs that a subordinate leader is to accomplish certain tasks by a certain time and, in some cases, by certain personnel. The subordinate leader errors when he or she does not tell the first sergeant if, for some reasons, he or she cannot complete

the task in accordance with first sergeants instructions. Deciding, for example, to use a different truck than the one specified, or a different soldier, is outside the bounds of the subordinate leader's authority. The subordinate leader makes a worse mistake in deciding that something else is more important, and the first sergeant instructions can be put on hold. Needless to say, priorities have shifted, and need to be realigned. All leaders understand that changes will be made to the best-laid plans. But when changes occur, the planner (in this case the first sergeant) must be informed if the mission or task cannot be accomplished as instructed.

- All of the first sergeant's frameworks of leadership. must be judiciously applied. Simply explained, what is good for one section or platoon is good for all. Once these frameworks are explained and understood, do not allow what is commonly referred to as "selective obedience".
- The unit itself as a structure must produce quality leaders. Yes, the Noncommissioned Officer Education System (NCOES is in place, allowing the unit to send soldiers off to learn while they wash their hands of their soldiers development—wrong answer. Your unit must have as many internal development programs as the mission will allow. Continuous development is one of the most important legacies that a first sergeant can leave his or her subordinate leaders. Ask yourself the question, "Does PLDC give a soldier all the basic leadership information that will last the entire military career?"
- All ethnic observances should receive the same amount of attention. Our diversified American culture requires that all leaders know something about the background of each minority group they lead—oriental, white, black, Indian/Native American, Puerto Rican, or Chicano. Know your soldier(s) and the contributions these diverse groups have made to the development of America.

Section V: Diamond Caring Principles

These principles, much like the management principles, must be published to ensure that your subordinate leaders know your priorities. Here are only a few of the "Diamond Caring Principles."

◊ Attempt to solve a soldier's problems at the lowest level. If you cannot solve the soldier's problems within the chain of command, elevate the problems.

◊ The fact that subordinate leaders cannot solve the soldier's problems is no reason to disregard the soldier's cry for help.

◊ The fact that there is a pressing mission is no reason for the subordinate leader to ignore the soldier's request for assistance. The soldier's request is a mission.

◊ The fact that the subordinate leader has a social function to attend is no reason to push aside the urgency of a soldier's problem that will not wait until tomorrow.

◊ Visits to your soldiers' quarters (on or off-post) are not just a command requirement. Visits are in the best interest of the soldier and his or her family. (See AR 623-205 • 15 May 2002)

Diamond Point: Subordinate leaders, inform their soldiers that they will be making visits to all soldiers' on and off-post quarters. Upon arrival, if the soldier is not home, wait only for a reasonable amount of time and leave a note.

◊ The hospitalization of a soldier or a family member must be of a greater leadership concern than it has ever been. It does not matter what the leadership does in addition to expressing their condolences to the soldier. Visiting in itself goes a long way in getting a good soldier to reenlist.

Diamond Point: Even though hospital visits come under the caring principle and even though it is said that leaders do not manage people—they lead them—there is a management side to the above. The hospital compiles information concerning hospitalizations. The hospital will also put you on the distribution list if requested. Make visits and ensure that the unit's subordinate leaders make their visits based on provided information. Have subordinate leaders inform the first sergeant when family members are hospitalized; from that provided information you can determine who you will visit.

◊ Learn the names of the children of some of the younger soldiers and occasionally ask, "How is Timmy doing?" Learning the names from any source other than the soldier is best. This technique can be used with any of the unit's soldiers, however, the real impact is with junior soldiers.

Diamond Point: If you really want to be good at the caring principles, find out the birthdates of the children and send out birthday cards. The first sergeant will have time to do this only for the good soldiers worthy of extra recognition.

◊ Enforce the philosophy that all soldiers below your grade belong to you. It does not matter that the soldier is not in your units squad or platoon; if the soldier is not being taken care of by his or her leaders, then the soldier belongs to you. If that soldier is out somewhere and needs help, do not ask who is his or her squad leader. That soldier, by virtue of what the leader wear and the fact that the soldier needs help, belongs to you.

◊ Ethnic observance is everybody's business. These observances are important to the soldiers as well as the unit. The families should always be invited to them.

This is a new school of thought that the future Corps must hold. The old school of thought was to determine who the leader was and have the leader take care of the matter by becoming involved.

Leaders need to love soldiers, no matter whose leadership they are under.

Diamond Point: The senior enlisted leadership, must adopt this as a standard, teach it, and then enforce it.

Diamond Point: The first sergeant also has an implied doing task that requires that the diamond wearer transform the mode of thinking of some of the senior leadership about certain sensitive subject i.e. ethnic observances, the Phantom's philosophy, etc.

Section VI: The Framework for Development

The framework for development includes anybody and everybody in the unit who needs to be developed. In maintaining contact with reality, the first sergeant must realize that there is always more to be learned within the command. One word of caution concerning the one-time teaching of a subject: NCODP is a continuous process requiring that certain classes be taught over and over during your tenure. The continuous turnover of personnel is another reason for a continuous program. The Nine Leadership Competencies have to be the core of your program.

A method that worked for me as the NCOs and I identified the content of our program was to use the most knowledgeable soldier for train-up. Another method was to have the violator of a military publication teach a class on the subject violated.

Examples:

a. If an NCO violated the provision(s) of AR 670-1, he or she gave a class on the proper wear of the uniform on the provision violated.
b. If, during formation, a subordinate leader incorrectly performed, then he or she would present the correct drill in accordance with FM 22-5.
c. If the NCO evaluation reports showed a lack of attention to detail as indicated by the numerous administrative errors, then an NCO would be selected to present a class using AR 623-205 (not always the Admin NCO).
d. Violators also taught classes on security, care of equipment, marksmanship, and field exercises (tactical).

Diamond Point: Note para. 3-3, AR 623-205 concerning the Nine Leadership Competencies.

Diamond Point: Development is one of the diamond wearer's watch words. No member of the unit escapes bit-of-advice that is always at the ready from the first sergeant's mental file.

Diamond Point: Development always carry with it the direct supervising and supporting tasks (DSSTs) and the follow on supervising and support tasks (FSSTs) concept. The first sergeant knows the correct position with regards to these concepts.

Section VII: The Framework for Evaluation

The unit's NCO must be taught that when systems fail, an evaluation must be conducted and corrective action applied. Hoping that by chance the situation will correct itself is dangerous management.

Force the NCOs to apply the problems and solvers.

Example 1:
> The best example that I can offer of the importance of this framework happened on or about my tenth month as first sergeant. After losing several good NCOs to situations of driving

after consuming alcohol, I decided to study the reasons that, after countless briefings, classes, and lectures, my senior soldiers were electing to tube any number of years. The command requirement was to hold classes and bring in experts to talk to the soldiers. Not any of these prevention actions helped me to turn the tide of DUIs or DWIs.

◊ I went back through the Serious Incident Files for about a year in making my evaluation, looking at various qualities of the soldiers who had fallen victim. I was trying to determine what more the command could do, short of holding all soldiers' hands 24 hours a day. I wanted something to jump out of those files and say, "Do this dummy."

◊ The solution was simple and one we could live with. I got the idea from a dying cancer patient who was being interviewed in her last hours. Also interviewed was her doctor, who talked about cancer in a way that I am sure was understood by the medical community. Here I was listening to two people talk about cancer, a cancer patient and a doctor. However, the effects were different. To a degree, I could relate to what the doctor was saying, but I could feel what she was saying.

◊ My experts then became NCOs whose lives had been changed by having one too many and then getting behind the wheel of a vehicle. There is a big difference in what a doctor can tell you about cancer and what a cancer patient can tell you about cancer. Most of the NCOs volunteered to share their nightmares for the benefit of their fellow NCOs. It all worked. I went from one alcohol-related driving incident a month to about one in six months. The effect of seeing the NCO unable to control his emotions while telling of the devastation he had endured was awesome. I did not care how much mucus flowed from his nose as he cried, I allowed him to continue in detail.

Example 2:

The training NCO was complaining that we were expending more ammunition than ever before for qualification, however, our qualification statistics were low. The platoon sergeants confirmed this with a follow-on statement that more personnel were going to the range than at this same time last year.

My analysis revealed the following:

◊ Soldiers who went to the range and failed to qualify returned to the unit, cleaned and turned in their weapons, and were simply rescheduled by the training NCO. No one asked what went wrong. Or, how many of those who went to the range qualified?

◊ No after-action review was conducted by the leaders to determine how to improve this negative situation. The leaders all looked at the training NCO as if it was his fault and he should present the solution to get these soldiers qualified.

Diamond Point #1: Just do not allow NCOs to pass the buck for substandard conditions, systems that fail, or soldiers out of uniform.

Diamond Point #2: Have the unit's NCOs openly share their failures with each other and find workable solutions. Their evaluations of themselves will prove valuable. If one soldier is lost to the judicial process, the matter becomes a matter of NCODP. One soldier's injury becomes a matter for all to evaluate/investigate.

CHAPTER V

DUTIES

Why do many fail:

Because they . . .

. . . fail to be sensitive to their worthiest instincts and feelings.

. . . fail to understand the nature of their trusteeship.

. . . fail to achieve the maturity of character that is expressed in the ability to make decisions, in putting aside that which is pleasant or unpleasant to him or her personally.

. . . fail the Phantom's Philosophy:

◊ Take care of the little guy
◊ Integrity above all
◊ Never do stupid things because of regulations or orders from them
◊ Chain of Command primary
◊ Community life is everybody's business
◊ Build for the long term
◊ Positive development to ensure equal opportunity
◊ Seek a better way
◊ Admit mistakes
◊ All acts rewarded or corrected as deserved
◊ Work friendly: enjoy your job

Diamond Point: A first sergeant has to have that greatness of the soul and truly love soldiers.

Diamond Point: Therefore, the diamond wearer engages in a day to day campaign to ensure that there are no blurring of training or soldier priorities, that there are needs analysis, that there are social-psychological strategies and other consistent mechanisms with failure prevention design.

Section I: Introduction to Duties

Many duties to be performed by the first sergeant are totally unrelated to those performed by the company commander. A few are shared: those are called overlapping duties and tasks.

The first sergeant's total understanding of specified, directed, and implied duties is crucial to the position. An effective first sergeant understands these three terms as they are applied not only to his or her position but also to the boss' position. This is the key to keeping the boss out of trouble and the mission of the unit on track.

Desk Bound . . .

. . . the world beyond your desk . . .

First sergeant, do not be a "desk jockey" or a "paper pusher" or a "super clerk," for those tasks are but a small fraction of your duties. You will have to push some paper. However, do not become a slave to the task. Allow only a portion of your daily schedule to be consumed pushing paper. Remember this, the longer you remain at your desk, the more paper will materialize, permitting your boss more time with your soldiers.

A few years back in this great Army of ours, there was talk of placing an admin NCO in each orderly room to relieve the first sergeant of much of the desk duty. The first sergeant would then be able to get out with the soldiers in their training. Moreover, the first sergeant needs to be out monitoring, mentoring, assessing, and evaluating unit training effectiveness, checking soldier morale, and ensuring that his or her frameworks of leadership are supported.

Diamond Point: The soldiers need to see their first sergeant and they will appreciate the interest in what they do in their worksites, their living quarters, and all aspects of their organizational life.

Understanding Duties . . .

. . . relating the first sergeant's duties to the commander's duties . . .

There could be at this point created a long laundry list of commander's specified duties (per Military Publications), but that is not the point of this section. The objective is to get you to understand the relationship of the first sergeant supporting duties to the commander's duties. Not all of the commander's specified duties will be spelled out or easily pulled from the written text. Likewise, you will not find an Army Publication where the commander's specified duties are delineated, followed by a line that says, "and these are the first sergeant's implied duties."

. . . supporting type duties . . .

First Sergeant's implied duties basically fall into two categories, those that support the commander's specified duties and those that support other first sergeant duties. At the point that implied duties become confusing, then go back to square one—the definition of an implied duty. Most of the first sergeant's implied duties are supporting duties. Very few of the first sergeant's implied duties are directed toward only the first sergeant doing tasks. This is what makes the first sergeant position so critically important.

The question that you must ask yourself is whether the commander will fail if this action is not accomplished. Is this a glass or rubber ball? In the back of your mind, keep telling yourself that Army regulations spell out the commander's specified duties and that he or she should be concerned with carrying out those duties. However, in the front of your mind, you should know that because of the number of specified duties Army Publications require the commander to accomplish, along with their directed and implied duties; the commander cannot do it all without some help.

... only three categories ...

All of the duties that a first sergeant performs must come under one of the three categories of duties. In the above paragraph, we established that the commander must have someone who is aware of his or her specified duties and also understands how to successfully complete these duties. Therefore, because the first sergeant is the assistant to the commander who ensures the accomplishment of the commander's specified duties, the first sergeant then takes on duties. How, then, does one classify these duties that the first sergeant takes on by virtue of the position? These duties cannot be classified as specified duties for the first sergeant, because they are not specified as such in the military publications. These duties are not directed duties because the system has not directed the first sergeant to perform these duties.

... into what category? ...

These duties fall into the implied duties category, covering all duties performed by a first sergeant that are not covered by the specified and directed duties. Even though these duties are not stipulated by an Army regulation or directed by someone in the chain of command, they are important enough to be made a part of the first sergeant's implied duties.

The specified duty of the commander is recast as an implied duty for the first sergeant, to show how it supports the accomplishment of the commander's specified duty. Below are some examples of the relationship of the two duties:

Example: AR 601-280

Commander's Specified Duty

Inspect the reenlistment data card file at least once a month to ensure that required interviews are being conducted and the *Total Army Retention* program is being administered properly.

First Sergeant Implied Duty

Ensure that the retention NCO provides the required reenlistment data cards. Schedule the interviews to ensure that they are conducted in a timely manner. Ensure that you understand the important aspects of the *Total Army Retention Program* so that it is administered properly.

Example: AR 601-280

Commander's Specified Duty

Unit commanders will ensure proper use by any soldier receiving an Enlistment Bonus (EB) or Selective Reenlistment Bonus (SRB).

First Sergeant's Implied Duties

◊ Maintain rosters of enlistment bonus and selective reenlistment bonus recipients.
◊ Inform commander when soldiers is not being properly used.

Again, the commander's specified duties are many, and not all of them will translate to implied duties for the first sergeant. That is not to say that the first sergeant should not be aware of these commander's specified duties. The truly successful first sergeant is one who knows many of the commander's specified duties and understands how to arrange and prioritize the first sergeant's supporting implied task.

Example: AR 601-280, para. 1-7e

Company, battery, detachment, or similar level commander's specified duties:

1. Maintain monthly, quarterly, and FY retention statistics.

2. Inspect the reenlistment data card file at least once a month to ensure that required interviews are being conducted and that the *Total Army Retention Program* is being administered properly.
3. Establish a *Total Army Retention Incentive Program* to recognize those persons who either reenlist, extend under the BEAR Program or enlist/transfer and accept an assignment in an RC unit.
4. Encourage maximum attendance at retention/transition ceremonies by persons who work with the soldier.
5. Ensure that additional duty unit retention NCOs are provided enough time to carry out their retention duties.
6. Provide the additional duty retention NCO enough time to attend retention training conducted by higher headquarters.

First Sergeant's Implied Duties

1. Mark calendar with due dates for statistics.
2. Work this task into commander's calendar and work around his leaves and other unit events.
3. Ensure that the incentive program is in place and enforced.

Example: AR 635-200
Insert yourself into the next four commander's specified duties as a drill to determine what the implied duties would be.

Commander's Specified Duties
Commander will ensure that adequate counseling and rehabilitative measures have been taken before initiating action to separate a soldier for one of the following reasons.

Commander's Specified Duties
AR 600-200, para 6-4 Inefficiency
The commander starting the reduction action will present documents showing the soldier's inefficiency to the reduction authority.

AR 614-200, para 7-18c
Commanders at any level may disapprove application for soldiers not meeting entry requirements. Applications so returned to the soldier must contain the specific criteria not met.

AR 614-200, para 8-18f

Commanders of active Army soldiers selected by HQDA for entry into the Drill Sergeant Program must ensure that the soldiers meet the requirements of this section.

Where there are specified duties for a commander, the first sergeant has to insert himself or herself into that commander's duty. Because of the myriad requirements placed on a commander, the importance can't be overstated of having a professional, competent, logistical, knowledgeable, self-motivated, and resourceful first sergeant.

You can help the commander to be successful in many ways. For example, para 1-4 (Responsibilities of Commanders) AR 623-205. Commanders are expected to ensure that . . .

1. Official rating schemes are published by name, and are posted in the unit so that all NCOs know their rater, senior rater, and reviewer; such schemes all include the effective dates of each rating official.

DISCUSSION: What is missing from the above statement is that the rating scheme should not or will not change without the knowledge of the commander. The biggest problem that will confront you is the change of NCO duty positions without the initiation of a DA Form 2166-8. Also ensure that everyone understands why the effective dates of each rating official are so important.

If the first sergeants would ensure these things are done, then relief for cause would be easier when required and fewer NCOER appeals would be made. The first sergeant is the NCOES system's watchdog.

When and if these things are not done, the commander shares the dereliction of the rating official.

2. Rating officials are fully qualified to meet their responsibilities and know who they are responsible to counsel, coach, and evaluate.

EXAMPLE: Even after the commander ensures that a copy of the regulation is available to the rated NCO and not the rating officials, the rating official will not ensure that the above is complied with. How does the rating official become fully qualified? How does the commander know when and if they are fully qualified to meet their responsibilities as rating officials? These are a few of the questions for which you will find very few answers.

Make it a habit of asking rating officials about their responsibilities as they are listed in the regulation.

Some of the questions you could ask the rating officials to determine their knowledge of the system are:

◊ What are the responsibilities of the rater?
◊ What are the responsibilities of the senior rater?
◊ Where would you find the responsibilities if you needed to know them, as a newly appointed official?
◊ What is the lowest ranking civilian who can perform the duties of a rater?
◊ Can the civilian be a rater who is officially designated on the published rating scheme established by the local commander?
◊ Can members of other U.S. military services be raters?
◊ Can members of Allied Forces be raters?

This raises only a few questions you could ask the officials. Moreover, if you ever ask an NCO who his or her rater or senior rater is and he or she does not know—consider separation.

Many of the younger commanders fail to understand the importance of para 1-4, Responsibilities of Commanders, by thinking that the NCOER is purely NCO business. Tell these commanders about their specified duties IAW AR 623-205 and that you are making them your implied duties.

Officers have to be experts on two and sometimes three evaluation systems—the officer's evaluation system, civilian system, and noncommissioned officers' evaluation system—because officers rate and senior rate NCOs, but NCOs do not rate officers. Because officers have to rate NCOs, there is an additional requirement for them to know the *NCO system* of evaluation. If they do not know the system and you, first sergeant assume that they do, you will have problems with your unit's evaluation system.

If and when the rating official takes this duty lightly, you must step forward to correct the situation.

First sergeant, the military system, must place on you the burden of monitoring, maintaining, and correcting procedures concerning the NCOER system. CSMs are too far removed to be as effective as the first sergeant can be. The real control level of this important NCO system lies in the hands of the power behind the throne. The real problem is that first sergeants do not understand this NCO system as well as they should.

3. Rating officials give timely counseling to subordinates on professionalism and job performance.

DISCUSSION: What is not included in the above duty is timely, *effective* counseling. This task has proven to be difficult for some command teams. Either the command team can go to the mountain—or have the mountain come to the command team. The only way the command team (Commander and the first sergeant) can ensure that the rating officials perform this task is to see the completed counseling, DA Form 2166-8-1. The rating official can bring the DA Form 2166-8-1 to your office or you can check them as you make your visit throughout the company area. You should inform the officials that failure to perform this vital task constitutes "dereliction of duty." Commanders should keep in mind that the senior rater has a part to play here. In the event the rater cannot perform, the senior rater has to perform the rater's functions (if qualified).

Diamond Point: First sergeant please understand in reading the senior rater's responsibilities that the rated NCO does not have to sign the DA Form 2166-8 if this form does not contain the counseling dates or correct dates.

4. Reports are prepared by the rating officials designated in the published rating scheme.

DISCUSSION: The rated soldier's first best argument for an appeal is that his or her report was not prepared by the rating officials designated in the published rating scheme. First sergeant, if you allow a report to be prepared that is not in keeping with the published rating scheme, then you should be ashamed.

Just do not allow changes until they have been cleared by the authority whose responsibility it is to ensure that reports are prepared by the rating officials designated in the published rating scheme. Also stress to your NCO Corps (leadership groups) that they should never allow their rater(s) to change duty positions without completing a DA Form 2166-8, provided the qualifications are met. It does not say much for the NCO Corps when a rated soldier points out that his rater changed six months ago. You can monitor the rating scheme from your position, but it is almost impossible to completely track the entire system all the time. Consider a scenario in which a rated soldier brings to the attention of the commander a report rendered by one of the subordinates in violation of AR 623-205 or not prepared by the designated rating official. What should be the commander's action? Throw the report out of the window with the rater. Rating officials often fail to understand the purpose of the published rating scheme and that the rating scheme cannot be changed at will.

Another significant problem that you will encounter concerning reports is the permanent change of station mismatch when either the rater or the rated soldier is gone for an extended period, for whatever reason, and either the rater or the rated soldier has to PCS. Build into your checks and balances for the internal system a series of questions that must be answered by both the rater and the rated soldier before anyone moves or goes anywhere. Likewise, if the rater or the rated soldier is not present when a report is required, some leaders will attempt to substitute rating officials to prevent late reports. It then becomes an integrity issue.

5. Rated NCOs are provided a copy of their completed evaluation report.

DISCUSSION: Up to this point we have discussed, for the most part, indirect actions of the commander dealing with the requirements of the rating officials. This task seems simple: just drop a copy of the completed DA Form 2166-8 into the distribution box, face up to the rated NCO. "Wrong!" Take a look at Chapter 6, AR 623-205, Administrative Instruction. The DA Form 2166-8 is the official document of the NCO Evaluation Reporting System. It contains evaluation information in the form of marked boxes and bullet comments that should be stored, handled, and transmitted as sensitive, personal information. Do not allow any DA Form 2166-8 to float around without the "Personal in Nature" folder.

You should work on establishing a standard routine in your unit for providing copies of the completed report to the NCO. One routine would be to place the completed report in an envelope (leave it open only if you place it in the soldier's hand). In some cases, the rated officials just do not care, but this discretion is a matter of understanding the NCO Evaluation Reporting System.

This reporting system starts with the DA Form 2166-8-1, NCOER Counseling Form, the mandatory face-to-face initial counseling that will culminate twelve months later with the completion of DA Form 2166-8, the NCOER. NCOs should not take a passive role in this process and accept, without their input, the completed DA Form 2166-8-1. If they do this, they are accepting the first installment of the short end of the stick.

Well-constructed statements of what the rated NCO is to accomplish during the rating period are the foundation of the counseling session. At the initial counseling, and every 90 days thereafter, NCOs should take an active role in adjusting the last counseling statements that were not well considered or well constructed. These adjustments also apply to statements that are directed too far above or below the NCO's level of competence, leadership, or training abilities.

Before the rater notifies the rated soldier of their counseling date, time, and place in accordance with the counseling guidelines in FM 22-101 and DA Form 2166-8-1, the NCO should make a list of tasks he or she will complete in addition to those the rater has targeted. If the NCOs do not take an active role in the process, they will receive the second installment of the short end of the stick.

The end of the rating period is too late for the NCO to pull his head out of the sand. The end of the rating period is too late to wave the flag of injustice and to tell the world your rater never counseled you, that he or she just told you to initial here.

... more implied duties ...

Another important specified duty of the commander or supervisors concerning promotions is found in paragraph 7-2c, AR 600-200.

Commanders or supervisors will counsel E5 and below soldiers who meet advancement or promotion eligibility, without waiver, but have not been recommended.

Because this task is in AR 600-200, it is a specified duty for the commanders or supervisors. And because the first sergeant is the commander's covering force, this task becomes an implied duty for the first sergeant.

It is not clear whether the regulation is stating that one or the other will or that if one does not, the other will. One way or another, E5 and below soldiers who meet advancement or promotion eligibility, without waiver, but have not been recommended *will* be counseled, so the commanders have been specified to ensure that the task is accomplished.

... getting subordinate leaders to see the intent of the regulation ...

The big question that should pop into your mind is how do you, this command team, ensure that soldiers are counseled? You can demand or direct that it be done, however, we might add that explaining to your subordinate leaders why it is important to counsel a soldier who meets advancement or promotion eligibility makes this task easier. A SGT (E5) or below who meets eligibility requirements must be told why, in no uncertain terms, the supervisor is not recommending the soldier for promotion. Also require that the counseling be face-to-face and be signed by both the supervisor and the soldier. Ensure that supervisors demonstrate their courage to tell a soldier what is wrong with his or her performance or potential.

The first sergeant is the overseer of the advancement or promotion eligibility system. If and when supervisors demonstrate a high state of judgment, then you, first sergeant, can accept their recommendations with a degree of certainty that you are advancing a quality soldier. This also will send another message to all elements of the unit proclaiming the effectiveness of the NCO Corps, and establishing the recommendations of the NCOs as a critical element in the operation of the unit.

AR 600-20 stresses the following:

As enlisted leaders of soldiers, NCOs are essential to furthering the efficiency of the company, battery, or troop.

However, for those supervisors who have demonstrated poor or no judgment on matters concerning their personnel, you must take a different approach toward their recommendations. If the subordinate leaders do not have the intestinal fortitude to tell a soldier why he or she will not be getting promoted, then the next-up leader must.

Diamond Point: First sergeant continue to stress the point that the term enlisted leader has taken on a different connotation today than that which it had a few years back. Great studies have been made in making the America noncommissioned officer corps the best in the world. Don't lose not one yard of ground in the battle of training. Once the NCOs have engulfed their implied skills, knowledge and attitudes in the continuous "learning cycle," they develop others to develop.

Section II: Dismounted Drill

Dismounted drill requirements or any type of battalion drill must be done and done well, and in accordance with FM 22-5. This is not to say that nothing else in the FM is important. If you have never had the opportunity to perform a company-level dismounted drill, do not wait until you have a high-level observer to fall on your face. All it takes to master this task is practice.

Newly appointed first sergeants have a problem making the platoon sergeant-to-first sergeant transition. They learned how to drill the platoon well, and will all too often push some young platoon sergeant aside to return to those familiar shores where they feel comfortable; done because the first sergeant cannot demonstrate company-level dismounted drill, he demonstrates what he knows (the platoon-level drills). Well, before the "diamond" is pinned on, you should study in detail all company elements in dismounted drill.

Even though you must be a student of the field manual on drill and ceremonies, the fundamentals of company drill require that you be a subject matter expert. The day of a special company drill is not the time to consult the field manual on drill and ceremonies to determine how to form a column from a company mass or form the company in column with platoons in line. The eyes of the future are upon you.

Become a subject matter expert on these chapters:

◊ Drill Instruction(s)
◊ Commands and Command Voice
◊ Individual Drill
◊ Individual Drill with Weapons
◊ Squad Drill
◊ Platoon Drill
◊ Ceremonies
◊ Saluting
◊ Manual of the Guidon
◊ Flags and Colors
◊ Manual of Arms—Automatic Pistols
◊ Terminology

The first sergeant position requires that you be the subject matter expert because at interactor stage 1 (squad leader level), you knew the drill and ceremonies as a squad leader; at interactor stage 2, you learned all that was to be learned about platoon drill; and now that you are at interactor stage 3, you need to know all the above as well as company drill.

Not knowing, and not bothering to know, will cause you problems. Seek every avenue to improve your knowledge of drill and ceremonies and you will be successful.

Dismounted drills that I had seen executed but had never performed myself were incorporated into my personal framework for learning. I was not too overcome by my position to ask one of my platoon sergeants, who had more knowledge of a particular drill, to give me a class. Find an open field away from your unit area and exercise your lungs. Practice until you feel comfortable with the drill. The next time you are required to execute that drill, you may be where the world is watching. You become comfortable with dismounted drill by practicing.

Diamond Point: There is too much in FM 22-5 for any one soldier to know it all. Practice! Practice! and require more practice!

Diamond Point: The first sergeant's direct supervising and supporting tasks (DSSTs) requires that the diamond wearer ensure that those at interactor stage 2 are trained to perform correctly.

Diamond Point: The diamond wearer also understands that even though the wearer does not directly train those at interactor stage 1, the first sergeant's follow-on supervising and support tasks (FSSTs) does require that he or she ensure that the platoon sergeant trains the squad leader to perform dismounted drills correctly.

Don't allow the voices of procrastination and failure to whisper negative thoughts into your ears.

Section III: Change of Command

Three to six months out is not too soon to begin planning the change of command, to ensure that it is above the standard expected. The below plan is just an example and does not contain as much detail as there should be. Word of warning: it is not wise to assume that anything will automatically happen.

Company Change of Command Checklist

D-6 months (for BN of higher) .... Set date, appoint points of contact.
(D-3 months for company)

D-5 months .... Determine and request required outside support.

D-3 months .... Select location, request facilities as appropriate for both outdoor and indoor locations. Order M16 magazines and padded chairs as necessary. Review FM 22-5.

D-80 days .... Select and coordinate equipment displays (if used).

D-50 days ....Order invitations, make guest list. Establish soldier practice plan*

D-30 days ....Coordinate refreshments, awards, and flowers. Present the outgoing commander the plans for review.

D-15 days ....Send out invitations. Second or third soldier drill practice.

D-10 days ....Outgoing commander approves plans. If he or she does not have the time to approve, go with them anyway.

D-3 days ....Training NCO walks ground and marks locations. Complete seating chart of guests who RSVPed.

D-2 days ....Key personnel rehearsal, both indoor and outdoor plans.

D-1 days ....Full dress rehearsal, to include marching on and off field.

D-1 Dress Rehearsal Checklist:

Uniformity: ....All M16s have magazines, and all are the same type (20 round vs. 30 round). All .45s have magazines, the same color lanyard, and same style holster. No special uniform for colorguards. No watches. No sunglasses, to include prescription photo-gray lenses. Identical LBE.

Narrator: ....Is well rehearsed. There should be at least one alternate narrator.

Ceremony: ....Have flowers and designated escorts for both spouses (incoming and outgoing). Rehearse the escorts completely at the key personnel and dress rehearsal.

* **NOTE:** The number of practices with the soldiers which you should specify depends on how often your soldiers get the opportunity to practice dismounted drill.

Section IV: NCO Proficiency

The proficiency of the NCO Corps affects the proficiency of the unit in all areas of operation. Let us discuss the connection of NCO proficiency and unit proficiency. Much of what happens, and the quality of those actions, depends on NCO proficiency.

NCO proficiency most definitely affects the unit's reenlistment program. When NCOs are knowledgeable of the program, they can better support the objectives and goals of the program.

... pecuniary activities ...

NCOs have to understand that their proficiency plummets when they engage in pecuniary activities with subordinates, i.e., selling, borrowing and/or lending money, etc.

... disciplined in ways befitting the rank ...

Any action that reduces the proficiency of the NCO will reduce unit proficiency as well. If you allow NCOs to be disciplined in ways not befitting their rank for breaches of conduct or substandard performance, you also are allowing a decrease in unit proficiency.

... making it make sense ...

August 20, 1986, Update: AR 600-20 listed a few duties required of the commander that the first sergeant needs to be aware of.

1. The commander will encourage harmonious relations among subordinates coupled with a friendly spirit of competition in performing duties ... encourage harmonious relations among subordinates ... Just what does that mean? Does it mean peer-to-peer or leader-to-subordinate, or does it leave it up to you to interpret? Internal teamwork is never overshadowed by that spirit of competition. When the unit steps forward as a unit, then internal teamwork is transformed to external teamwork. Considering the unit diversity and many different missions, everyone must understand that for no reason will any section of the unit be allowed to fail.

... why of harmonious relations ...

Wisdom comes in knowing before the mission is assigned where repairs in the harmonious relations are needed. Why is it important for the commander to encourage harmonious relations? Have you ever seen units or been assigned to units that tried to maintain or accomplish missions well without harmonious relations (subjective combat effectiveness indicators)?

... force merging NCOs ...

Your NCOs will not get to know each other during the day-to-day operations. The best and quickest way to merge them is to plan social functions that they all would be required to attend. NCO call is where all NCOs (CPL and above) are allowed to talk and be heard regardless of position. Remember that talking about it all is half the battle. NCOs are in the unit for as long as three years and the only other NCOs they know are the ones within their work circle. Social gatherings not only build unity, but also encourage harmonious relations.

... commander's duties connecting NCO duties ...

If you think paragraph 5-7a was thought-provoking, take a look, at paragraph 5-7b, which reads: The commander's timely intervention to prevent disputes, give advice to the inexperienced, and censor conduct that may produce dissension in the command or reflect discredit upon it, is of great importance in securing and maintaining efficiency ... timely intervention to prevent disputes. Please make me smarter! Is this to prevent disputes between peers or disputes between supervisors and subordinates or does it leave it up to us to interpret? In order to keep the harmonious-relations status in perspective, disputes between peers we can understand.

The next paragraph is easy to understand and interpret for it's reduced to a message that leaders use each day. Paragraph 5-7c: Commanders exercise command through their subordinate commanders. To this end, they inspire confidence in subordinates by example, sound and decisive action, and ability to overcome obstacles. Commanders must encourage strengthening the chain of command and developing initiative, ingenuity, and boldness of execution throughout all echelons of command.

And because the commander has to identify enlisted members of the command and advise them on their rights and responsibilities to the service, there is a part for you to play in this commander's specified task.

DISCUSSION:

You should ask yourself what the rights and responsibilities are? Too many of our soldiers today do not fully accept the fact that the Army comes first. In order to explain in detail, you have to know the "whos" and the "whys."

Ensure that when soldiers are counseled, all important data is collected and the counseling did take place, according to the provisions of paragraph 5-29, a-f AR 600-20. First sergeant, understand that while receiving counseling, some of your young soldiers will not understand the involuntary separation provisions in AR 635-200, para 5-8 (. . . could be carried out whenever parenthood interferes with military responsibilities).

When the commander speaks of AR 601-280, chapter 6, and about a bar to reenlistment for failure to provide an approved Family Care Plan, or for failure to manage family affairs, your young soldier(s) will not fully understand what that bar to reenlistment means.

Any action, policy, directive, LOI, SOP, regulation, or manual that limits, decreases or prohibits the proficiency of the NCO should be elevated and dealt with accordingly. The author of any such document has not considered the effect on overall efficiency by limiting, decreasing, or prohibiting NCOs' proficiency.

. . . anti actions . . .

First sergeants all have to understand that limiting, decreasing, or prohibiting NCOs' proficiency, is anti-Army. Because the greatest portion of our Army consists of NCOs, behavior or action that is not designed to stimulate, revitalize, or modify the NCO proficiency is anti-Army.

Simply put, do not allow this drain on efficiency by these self-appointed crusaders. Some, made of "human stuff," despise NCOs simply because they are NCOs. They aim for the NCO, not really understanding their full impact. Your years of experience will show you that these usually are lower achievers.

. . . upholding standards of dignity . . .

When confronted with lapses of dignity, always be willing and ready to fall upon the sword in defense of the Corps and enjoy doing it. Be willing to stand and be counted as an upholder of the standards of dignity. Your failure to put a stop to these counter-productive actions will be viewed by your leadership groups as "selling out" the corps. Leadership is not easy—it never was meant to be.

If the chain of command does not respond to your reports of "soldier inhumanity to soldier," the IG is on your side.

Diamond Point #1: Falling on your sword is a learned art. You have got to know when and where to perform the act.

Diamond Point #2: Shielding the enlisted population is one of your cardinal principles.

... founded on the dignity of man ...

Consistently, from the time of the Colonies, this nation has abhorred press gangs, floggings, group punishment, martinetism, and all of the other old-world military practices that demean the rank and file. Our military system was founded on the dignity of man just as was our Constitution. The system has sought always to advance by appealing to the higher nature of the individual. That is why the commissioned people need to be gentle folk. To call forth steadfast loyalty in others and to enlist it in any high endeavor, one must first be sensible of their worthiest instincts and feelings. (The Armed Forces Officer, 1975 edition, pages 3 and 4).

Diamond Point: Ensure that their task is accomplished of calling forth that steadfast loyalty in others.

Priority Conflicts ...

... unhealthy friction ...

Even though the company's officers will rate the NCOs and the NCOs will work directly for the officers, the mentoring and developing of the NCO corps belongs to you. However, remember what we said about the Byzantines' Emperor. You create many things in the unit, but friction between NCOs and their officers should never be one of your creations. Nor do you want to threaten the tenuous link between you and the officers, creating conditions that would limit the latitude of your young officers. There will be conflicts when you direct an action and the platoon leader directs another counter action. Power plays are not healthy unit builders, but are sometimes required to get the message across.

... commander's priority ...

The best way to defuse the conflict is to consider the commander's intent. Both the officers and the NCOs (the leadership groups) should be focused on the priority set forth by the commander. All the submissions should be focused on accomplishing the unit's mission.

The subordinate leader should never be left to defend a conflict created or generated by opposite directives. Once you become aware that a subordinate leader is caught in the middle of a power play, you must step forward and resolve the issue even if that requires the commander's involvement.

Diamond Point: Soldiers will look to you to work them out of these conflicts.

Pecuniary Activities . . .

The first sergeant should ensure that all the NCOs understand that their proficiency drops when they engage in pecuniary activities with subordinates. Nothing is wrong with a legal transfer of property from subordinate to leader or leader to subordinate, but it must not happen too often. Problems arise with these dealings when the offer is made to "pay later." When an NCO accepts property from a soldier without paying, the NCO then "owes" that soldier. Outside the professional arena, NCOs cannot owe soldiers anything, even if the soldier agrees that the NCO "pays later."

. . . when soldiers "get something" on your NCOs . . . Proficiency of your NCOs is further decreased when a soldier "gets something" on an NCO. The soldiers know who is "out there" and what they are doing. Even a rumor is enough to call an NCO in for a face-to-face session. When you give that strong, up-front warning, there should be no doubt in the mind of the violator that no mercy will be shown. Once that task has been accomplished, you need to make note of the date, time, and points of interest. The credibility of the information should help you determine whether the face-to-face should be put in writing.

Diamond Point #1: Have one of your NCOs who have violated the restrictions on Private Activities give a class on FM 27-14.

Diamond Point #2: Your leadership groups must understand that it is hard to give a soldier orders if that soldier has "something" on them.

Diamond Point #3: The first sergeant must seek out this violation of trust and all such situations deteriorating teamwork in the unit.

Diamond Point #4: The first sergeant should in a coordinated effort with the command sergeant major recommend an organized policy letter outlining the "do's" and "dont's" of trading.

Dealing With Incompetence and Inefficiency . . .

Incompetence and inefficiency are not pleasant subjects but ones that you must discuss and be aware of as NCOs.

. . . defined . . .

Incompetence is defined as the state of being poorly qualified, or incapable. An incompetent soldier is inadequate for his or her purpose, unsuitable; insufficient.

Inefficiency is demonstrated when a person cannot perform the duties and responsibilities of the grade and MOS. Inefficiency may include any conduct that clearly shows the soldier lacks the abilities and qualities normally required and expected of an individual of that grade and experience (AR 600-8-19).

. . . forefront subject . . .

Incompetence must be one of the subjects of your NCODP program and is one that our service schools should include in the curriculum. Many of our NCOs failures are due, in part, to our lack of highlighting subjects such as incompetence. Incompetence is allowed to thrive because you, the leadership, tolerate it. Whenever incompetence is discussed, the relief for cause must be a sub-topic.

A constant assessment of the NCO corps will help you separate the performers from those who lack the ability to perform.

. . . shielding incompetence . . .

Young officers will often shield incompetent NCOs by not allowing them the opportunity to demonstrate their incompetence. Once incompetence is demonstrated, then it can be dealt with. In your framework for leadership is that NCO task of counseling and documenting attempts to rehabilitate.

Diamond Point: Your leaders must understand that before a label is placed on a soldier, that soldier must have had sufficient time to earn that label. Leadership groups must know that once a soldier is branded, brands are not easily removed.

Section V:

Debts: AR 600-15 . . .

Leadership is still the best aid for solving soldiers' debt problems. There is no better guide than AR 600-15, Indebtedness of Military Personnel, to answer the following questions:

◊ How do you explain to your soldiers that the failure to pay their debts promptly and to manage their personal affairs affects the soldier as well as the Army's public image?

◊ What is the Army's position concerning judging or settling disputed debt claims, creditors, and debt collectors?

◊ What action(s) should be taken by the command team regarding complaints of repeated failure to pay debt claims or lack of effort to resolve unpaid debts promptly by a soldier(s)?

◊ What type of protection and relief of individuals with a regular income does Chapter XIII of the bankruptcy act (II USC 1301, et. seq.) offer?

◊ How does the failure to pay debts honorably and promptly affect official personnel files?

◊ What should be done with debt complaints received against soldiers no longer on active duty, retired, or former soldiers of your unit?

Diamond Point #1: Soldiers as well as leaders must understand that being in debt is not a crime. The crime is the failure to pay honorably and promptly.

Diamond Point #2: Ensure that your admin soldiers (clerks) understand and comply with the rules of releasing information, the Privacy Act of 1974, and infringing on the rights of the soldier(s).

Diamond Point #3: Indebtedness or disputed debt claims can get messy. The Staff Judge Advocate (SJA) is there for guidance.

Section VI: The School of the Soldier

The following is an article that appeared in DA Pam 27-50-10, June 1981, concerning a subject that you can always welcome guidance on, "The School of the Soldier."

In the over two hundred years since the establishment of the republic, millions of servicemen have promptly and proficiently responded to the commands of their superiors in both war and peace. This commendable history has been the result of the intensive inculcation into the soldier of the basic requirements of military skills and discipline. When a serviceman proves himself deficient in either or both of these areas, the commander may, if so desired, resort to administrative, nonjudicial, or judicial punishment to right the perceived wrong. Alternatively, a commander may instead opt to order extra training for the soldier as a remedy for the military deficiency. As such a course of conduct constitutes training, a legitimate command goal, and not punishment, resort to formal action is not required and no permanent record is to be made of the episode.

Perhaps the most popular yet controversial form of "additional training" is commonly known as the "school of the soldier." Typically, the school of the soldier held on a non-duty day, most frequently weekends, and consists of a scheduled program of instruction and training in basic military skills, e.g., in ranks uniform and equipment inspections, drill and ceremonies, physical training, and military courtesy. To the extent that such activity requires an intrusion upon the otherwise free time of the serviceperson, it certainly must seem to the soldier to constitute punishment. From the viewpoint of the command, however, the "school of the soldier" is seen as a simple military remedy for simple military problems diagnosed in the soldier. It is the purpose of this article to discuss the legality of an order that a service member attend the "school of the soldier."

I.   The Problem

Article 13 of the Uniform Code of Military Justice (UCMJ) provides that "no person, while being held for trial or the result of trial, may be subjected to punishment or penalty other than arrest or confinement upon the charges pending against him . . ." If an individual is to be punished, he must first be afforded the rights and safeguards provided by the process attending the imposition of nonjudicial punishment or trial by court-martial. Thus, an order by a commander to a service member to perform punishment prior to a proper adjudication of his case is illegal and need not be obeyed. If, however, the order is construed as one to perform a legitimate form of extra training, then it will be deemed to "relate to military duty" and disobedience of it will be punishable under the UCMJ. The issue is therefore narrowed as to whether a direction to a service member to attend the school constitutes an illegal order to perform punishment or a legal order to perform remedial training.

II. What is Training?

The seminal case involving remedial training is United States vs. Trani. In Trani, a 1952 decision, a confined prisoner intentionally destroyed certain prison records. The prison officer thereupon directed the prisoner to perform close order drill during normal duty house until he "shaped up and got a little better discipline, better control of himself." The accused declined to obey the order and was tried and convicted for his disobedience. The Court of Military Appeals sustained the conviction. In addressing the issue of the validity of the order, the court explained that "the command of a superior officer is clothed with a presumption of legality, and that the burden of establishing the converse devolves upon the defense." With the burden of proof thus stated, the court determined that the defense failed to meet it. Recognizing that a commander should be permitted "generous latitude in diagnosing ills and prescribing remedies," the panel could not find a lack of "colorable relationship" between the perceived shortcoming of the accused, i.e., absence of discipline and self-control, and the cure selected, i.e., a traditional form of military training which the commander credibly and sincerely believed to constitute training and not punishment. Absent a clear showing of unlawfulness, the order to perform this type of activity was found to be valid.

III. What is Punishment?

The courts have provided more guidance concerning what is not remedial training. If the assigned "training" is in fact detail-type work such as might be imposed by nonjudicial punishment or court-martial, then there is little doubt that it will be labelled as punishment. In United States vs. Reeves, for example, the accused was gigged in morning formation and instructed by his first sergeant to mow the lawn as "extra instruction." The court readily found that this duty was an illegally imposed punishment. Similarly, an after-hours barracks cleanup detail and a kitchen police detail were also deemed to be punishment rather than training. Orders designed to humiliate the "trainee" bear the earmarks of punishment as well. In United States vs. Raneri, the accused deposited two parachutes on the floor of a parachute loft in a manner deemed improper by the parachute rigger. The accused was then instructed to pick up the parachutes and proceed from shop to shop in the hanger. At each location, he was to properly lay the parachutes down and announce to all present that "this is the correct way to handle and carry parachutes." The accused was court-martialed for his refusal. On appeal, the court determined that the order was designed to serve no purpose other than the "direct and immediate punishment" of the accused. The seeming humiliation of the accused which would have resulted from his obedience of this order amply rebutted the presumption of legality. Finally, the integration of the "trainee" with those undergoing judicially or nonjudicially imposed punishment will serve to invalidate the order. In United States vs. Bayhand, the accused, a prisoner awaiting trial, was assigned to the same work details, while working the same hours, subject to the same instructions, and wearing the same garb as sentenced prisoners undergoing punishment. That the accused was also being punished was the inescapable conclusion.

IV.   School of the Soldier: Some Guidelines

The Department of the Army has issued some suggested guidelines for properly applied corrective training.

a.   An individual appearing in improper uniform may be required to attend special instruction in correct wearing of the uniform.
b.   An individual in poor physical shape may be required to take additional conditioning drills and participate in extra field and road march exercises.
c.   An individual who has unclean personal or work equipment may be required to devote additional time and effort to clean the equipment and be given special instruction in its maintenance.
d.   An individual who executes drills poorly may be given additional practice drill.

e. An individual who fails to maintain his housing or areas in proper condition or who abuses property may be required to perform additional maintenance leading to a correction of his shortcoming.

f. An individual who fails to perform properly in his assigned duty may be given special formal instruction or additional on-the-job training in those duties or skills relating to them to correct his performance.

g. An individual who is deficient in responding to orders may be required to participate in additional drills and exercises to develop his responsiveness to the prompt execution of orders.

From the foregoing, it is apparent that a relationship should exist between the ailment and the cure. It is submitted, however, that these guidelines are not restrictive than the contours of the law. The Trani case clearly affords the commander a considerable discretion in fashioning a "colorable relationship" between the deficiency and the corrective training. Thus, insofar as the commander determines that the appearance of a soldier in improper uniform, or in poor physical condition, or with unclean equipment may be indicative of a lack of self-discipline, motivation, or attentiveness to the basic requirement of military life, the soldier may be required to attend the full gamut of school of the soldier instruction. Similarly, the soldier deficient in basic military skills may be deemed to require a re-introduction to those skills in which he is weak as well as the fortification of those areas in which he is strong.

The restrictions of such a program are obvious. The schedule activities should involve traditional forms of military training in basic military traits and skills; detail-type work is to be avoided. The trainees should perform their training as a group and apart from soldiers undergoing punishment. The training should be highly motivated and, above all, conducted in a professional manner. Care should be taken by commanders to select for the school of the soldier only those service members who are deficient in motivation, discipline, or military skills and knowledge. Thus, while the disrespectful, disobedient, sloppy, or careless soldier might qualify for inclusion in the program, the "colorable relationship" dims when soldiers who are suspected of common law crimes, e.g., assault, larceny, or drug offenses, are included. It can easily be imagined that a court might conclude that, traditionally, deficient soldiers are trained; criminal ones are punished.

Properly utilized, the school of the soldier would permit the commander to take full advantage of the discretion afforded him by law in exercising that degree of leadership necessary to make good soldiers from seemingly bad ones. Once remedied, the shortcoming of the soldier would be forgotten, not memorialized. Abused, such a program would keep the inspectors general burning the midnight oil. As always, it is the responsibility of the local judge advocates to constantly review the operation of the "school of the soldier" in those jurisdictions in which it has been established.

DISCOM SCHOOL OF THE *SOLDIER* PROGRAM OF INSTRUCTION

TIME	SUBJECT	UNIFORMS	INSTRUCTOR	REFERENCE	LOCATION
0645-0700	Roll Call (Muster)	Class A	Sr Cadre	Inst Notes	TBA
0700-0750	SPS Brief/ Inspection in Ranks			AR 60-1 FM 22-5	TBA
0750-0815	Break & Chg Uniforms	Class A	Cadre	Div Policy	
0815-0900	Insp/Proper Wear of Uniforms	Duty	Cadre	Div Policy	Unit Area
0900-0950	Breakfast	Duty	Cadre	Div Policy	Unit Area
0950-1000	Break	Duty	Cadre	Div Policy	Unit Area
1000-1050	D & C	Duty	Cadre	FM 22-5	Unit Area
1050-1100	Break	Duty	Cadre	Div Policy	Unit Area
1100-1150	Wear of MOPP Gear Mask	Duty w/	Cadre	Div Policy	Unit Area
1150-1250	Break/lunch	Duty	Cadre	Div Policy	
1250-1300	Form w/TA 50	Kelvar/LBE	Cadre	Inst Notes	M WRNS
1300-1315	Enrte TA 50 Layout Area	Kelvar/LBE	Cadre	Inst Notes	Bayonet Field
1315-1445	Prep & Insp of Layout	Duty	Cadre	Fig 2-5	Field
1445-1515	Recover TA 50	Kelvar/LBE	Cadre	Field	
1515-1530	Prep for PT Secure TA 50	PT	Cadre	Field	
1530-1630	PT & Retreat	PT/Duty	Cadre	FM 21-20	T & 2mi
1630-1650	Counseling Indiv Critique	Duty	Cadre		
1650-1700	Secure TA 50 & Rtn to Unit	Duty	Cadre Notes		Unit Area

As long as the best interest of the Army is served and our focus is on good order and discipline, we are doing what we should as leaders.

The "School of the Soldier" is one of the NCO's methods of ensuring good order and discipline with an alternative of requesting nonjudicial punishment.

The following is an article that appeared in DA Pam 227-50-102, June 1981, that will help shed some light on the subject concerning gifts, coercion, and the compliance with D.O.D. Regulation 5500.7-R, Joint Ethics Regulation. See also the Joint Ethics Regulation—DOD Regulation.

GIFTS, COERCION, AND
IMPROPER USE OF GOVERNMENT ASSETS

1. A recent Department of the Army investigation highlighted the problems which may arise when commands fail to enforce the limitations applicable to the acceptance of gifts by superiors from subordinates and the use of Government assets for unofficial purposes. The investigation also surfaced problems arising from the use of coercive methods on behalf of fund-raising or membership campaigns of private groups. This letter provides general guidance so that future problems can be avoided.

2. Generally, Department of the Army personnel may not solicit a contribution from other DOD personnel for a gift to an official superior, make a donation as a gift to an official superior, or accept a gift or contribution from other DOD personnel subordinate to themselves (See Joint Ethics Regulation). However, an exception to this policy permits truly voluntary gifts of nominal value or contributions of minimal value of "special occasions" such as marriage, transfer, illness, or retirement.

Any gift acquired with such contributions must not exceed a nominal value.

   a. Whether a gift is truly voluntary depends upon the facts involved. Collection methods such as making individual assessments, using lists of contributors or non-contributors for purposes other than accounting for funds, and making repetitious requests for donations would all be indicative of involuntary contributions or gifts.

b. Gifts of nominal value are those of a sentimental nature, with little or no intrinsic value to anyone other than the recipient. Intrinsic value is determined by the essential nature of the gift. While inexpensive plaques or trays normally would be permissible, items such as pistols, shotguns, gun cabinets, coffee tables, or silver service sets would be improper.

3. It is improper to use or allow the use (either directly or indirectly) of Government property, facilities, or manpower in the manufacture or preparation of gifts for DOD personnel and their dependents. (See Joint Ethics Regulation.) This prohibition would preclude the use of the installation carpentry shop, training aides facility, or self-service supply center in the fabrication of gifts for "special occasions." It also applies even though "scrap" material is used, or a private organization (flower and cup fund) or an individual supplies the material. On the other hand, because this prohibition is aimed at insuring that appropriated funds are used in a manner and for the purpose for which intended there would be no objection to a skilled volunteer who is an eligible patron occasionally using off-duty time to prepare a gift such as a wood plaque while utilizing the installation Morale Support Activity craft shop.

4. Commands should ensure that Department of the Army policy is followed in supporting the activities, membership efforts, and fund raising campaigns of various private associations which are recognized as beneficial to the Department of the Army.

a. Membership in such organizations must be truly voluntary. Practices that involve or give the appearance of involving compulsion, coercion, influence, or reprisal must be avoided. This prohibition includes the following: repeated orientations, meetings, or similar methods of counseling personnel who have chosen not to join; using membership statistics in support of supervisory influence (e.g., comparing units on the basis of percentage of membership in a particular private association; and compilation of by-name lists of nonmembers).

b. Commands also must avoid all activities that involve or imply Department of the army sponsorship of such organizations of their activities. For example, it would be improper for a commanding general to send an official letter to the command which states that he or the Army endorses a certain private association. However,

THE DIAMOND, SECOND EDITION

commanders are permitted to use reasonable efforts to inform or encourage personnel, without coercion, regarding the benefits and worthiness of such organizations (See Joint Ethics Regulation).

c. Department of the Army policy concerning official support of fund-raising activities is specified in AR 600-29, Fund Raising Within the Department of the Army, and AR 360-61, Community Relations.

5. While certain private organizations, such as wives clubs, may be authorized to operate on Department of the Army installations, official support to such organizations is generally limited to providing meeting space. AR 210-1, Private Organizations on Department of the Army Installations, should be consulted before furnishing other items of logistical support. Informal unorganized groups, such as senior officers' wives coffee circles, which lack formal authorization to operate on installations, generally are not authorized to receive logistical support. Individual members of such a group may, of course, arrange for meeting space at an Army club facility.

6. Commanders recently were urged by HQDA to seek advice and assistance of their staff judge advocates to ensure that all actions taken by them involving gifts, use of Government assets, and support to private organizations' membership campaigns and fund-raising activities are in accordance with governing policies. I am confident that all staff judge advocates will be alert for potential problems in this area and swift to provide expert guidance and assistance. Staying within these guides will help us maintain command climates that enhance good order and discipline.

Section VII: Family Mediator

Family mediation requires a great deal of caution. You cannot and must not in any way be a part of the decisions made by the husband nor the wife. You must do a great deal of listening. Your objective on these family matters is simply to help them settle their differences, even to seek professional help.

. . . getting the dialogue started . . .

Do not, and I repeat do not, give any advice that you are not qualified to give. The first step is just to defuse the negative situations that are disreputable to the command. Defuse negative situations by getting the dialogue started between the people involved. As these people begin to talk and decide what their options are, you have accomplished your objective.

... personal matters becoming community matters ...

Inform the military member that his or her family matters become community matters when the family can no longer control family situations, and that the command will not tolerate these negative family situations. Explain to the military member that there is professional help available and that the command will do everything within its power to help them through this situation, but the command will not tolerate these negative family situations. The command's desire is always that the family solve family matters. The family member should get a clear understanding that if he or she does not solve the problem, then the command will take steps to solve the matter.

... commander and professional involvement ...

Matters of serious nature (family rape, family abuse, marital conflict) require that the commander become involved, however, for the most part, less serious family matters can be resolved by the diamond wearer, who should inform the commander. Professionals who have been trained in the matters of social problems know how to defuse negative situations, so you should not hesitate in getting them involved. To allow three or more of your days, which could be spent with your soldiers, to be spent trying to convince or reason with a spouse in counterproductive. Soldiers involved in one-time occurrences should be counseled in writing that matters of family are family matters until these matters require command involvement.

The Family Advocacy Program ...

The Family Advocacy Program (FAP) has as its objective the prevention of child and/or spouse abuse by encouraging the reporting of all instances of abuse to ensure the prompt investigation, protecting victims of abuse, and treating all family members affected by abuse so that those families can be restored to a healthy state. In carrying out these objectives, the FAP will:

a. Provide installation commanders staff assistance in addressing the problems of spouse and child abuse.

b. Prevent spouse and child abuse through information and education.

c. Provide services to at-risk families who are vulnerable to the kinds of stresses that can lead to abuse.

d. Identify abuse as early as possible in order to prevent further injury.

e. Provide treatment services to soldiers and their families involved in family violence in order to strengthen the family and prevent the reoccurrence of abuse.

f. Encourage voluntary self-referral through education and awareness programs.

Leaders at all levels need to learn these directives for we know not where abuse will raise its ugly head. Abuse is leaders' business.

. . . all leaders' involvement . . .

Because abuse is leaders' business, the unit leadership should digest the objectives of the FAP. You are required to get involved in the program for the prevention, reporting, investigation, and treatment of child and spouse abuse as outlined in AR 608-18, The Army Family Advocacy Program.

The Army FAP outlines the specified duties of the unit commanders. These duties include, but are not limited to, the following:

a. Attend spouse and child abuse command education programs designed for unit commanders. Ensure first of all that your commander attends and shares the information or attend yourself. This duty also will compete for the command team's valuable time.

b. Schedule time for soldiers to attend troop awareness briefings.

c. Be familiar with rehabilitative, administrative, and disciplinary procedures relating to spouse and child abuse. You do not need to wait until you have one of these situations to become familiar with these procedures.

. . . investigating suspected cases . . .

Prevention in ounces is worth pounds of cure. Spouse or child abuse is a negativism that you and the commander should pursue. Any and all reported or suspected cases must be investigated. Soldiers do not function as well as they can if their home life is not what it should be.

Diamond Point #1: In your investigations keep in mind that the soldier himself or herself could be the abused one.

Diamond Point #2: Putting your head in the sand concerning these matters could result in a death.

Section VII: Eradicator/Exterminator

... separating can be wasteful ...

Problem soldiers who cannot or will not perform their duties effectively have been with us since the beginning and will be with us for years to come. They continue to occupy a significant amount of the leadership's time. The administrative options available range from moderate to more severe actions. First sergeant, the most drastic and severe action is separating the soldier from the Army. Separating your problem soldiers can be wasteful and sometimes unfair. You have to ensure that it is done right.

... degrading the corps ...

You must be the eradicator/exterminator of substandard NCOs. Identify them and then send them on to jobs that will better accommodate their life style. The NCO Corps is just not their calling in life and you owe them assistance in finding their callings elsewhere. All the bleeding hearts need to understand that this time-honored profession is not designed for some. By allowing substandard soldiers to remain on active duty who have neither the desire nor the ability to improve, you degrade the Corps and its image. Part of your commitment is ensuring that the example is set.

Allowing the heart to bleed will cause you problems in the long run.

... they show up everywhere ...

How can we identify this group? They are not hard to identify. They are just as noticeable as the group that upholds the standards. Here are some of the places you will find them and ways in which they stand out.

◊ In any military or civilian air or bus terminal anywhere in the world. They are the ones wearing the black all-weather coat improperly while in uniform.
◊ The soldier in the shopping area whose Army greencoat does not extend below the crotch or fit easily over the chest and shoulders.
◊ At the NCO Club wearing a windbreaker not zipped up at least three-fourths of the way.
◊ Sitting in an office wearing the shirt, AG 415, long sleeve, without the four-in-hand necktie.

◊   Walking across a post with a map bag strapped across his or her shoulder while in uniform.

◊   During physical fitness formations, wearing earrings.

Diamond Point: It is you, the NCO Corps, who must clean up the NCO Corps.

... counseling as a corrective tool ...

Your leadership groups (subordinate leaders) will much too often substitute verbal counseling for what should be written counseling. This occurs because only with experience will the leader be able to find the right words to fit the violated situation.

The following are some examples of introduction statements for NCO negative counseling:

Circumstances

◊   Failure of an NCO to play an extremely important role in furthering the efficiency of this unit.

◊   Failure to emphasize the important status of an NCO in maintaining discipline in the Army.

◊   Provided for his/her own comfort and personal advancement at the expense of others.

◊   Cannot (or) does not have the ability (or) need to improve his/her ability to deal with others in a respectful manner.

◊   Has not developed a program of learning to keep himself/herself abreast of current developments in his military specialty, command policies, and the local and/or world communities.

◊   Lacks the ability or desire to improve his or her ability to logically weigh facts and possible solutions on which to base sound decisions.

◊   Lacks uprightness and soundness of moral principles or the quality of truthfulness and honesty. Lacks unquestionable integrity.

◊   Lacks the ability to deal with a situation in the absence of normal resources or methods.

◊   Lacks the mental and physical stamina measured by the ability to withstand pain, fatigue, stress, and hardship.

◊   Lacks the voluntary compliance with directives and regulations of leaders whose requirements are established in the interests of the organization.

Diamond Point: Writing negative counseling that in fact has important information a soldier can use must be part of your program of learning.

... subordinate leader breaking bonds to make correction ...

First sergeant, your subordinate leadership groups may have problems telling a soldier why he or she will not appear before a promotion board. These subordinate leaders, for whatever reason, cannot look a soldier in the eye and say—no. Two chief reasons for this squeamishness are the leader's poor performance counseling and personal working relations. Too many subordinate leaders are personal friends with those they supervise.

Soldiers will also play games with younger, less experienced leaders by walking the straight line long enough to get recommended or promoted, and then returning to their old ways.

You, first sergeant, have to ensure that the leadership training takes in as a subject "Reading the Soldier."

Section IX:

Organic Personnel ...

The normal trend of first sergeant leadership has been a to go easy on those closest to the throne, the organic-personnel. That old school of thought has been "scudded" by present-day leaders for a more modern point of view. These high-quality soldiers postulate that all soldiers are to perform to standard and none will be excused.

... days of disrespectful clerks are gone ...

The days of the unit's head clerk telling NCOs where they could go and how fast they could get there are gone. It is agreed by our present day leaders that a sense of alertness, urgency, and attention to detail must be instilled in all of your soldiers—you owe them that. The days of allowing an orderly room clerk to be disrespectful and place statements of disrespect in a first sergeant's desk drawer are gone. Discipline is every soldier's right. Leaders must ensure that they get plenty of discipline. The days are gone when unit NCOs were afraid to correct soldiers who worked for the first sergeant.

... setting the highest standards ...

The organic personnel under your control should be the example of good soldiering, standard enforcers not standard breakers. Therefore, you should have programs of discipline as well as programs of learning for your organic personnel.

Supply Sergeant . . .

. . . surveys too often mean money out of soldiers' pockets . . .

Many Reports of Survey amounting to more dollars than we care to count have been leveled against NCOs, many of which are or were supply sergeants. It is astounding that many of these surveys are not due to inefficiency but to unavoidable malassignments and reclassification of NCOs. None-the-less, monies that these soldiers need to support their families are deducted from their pay because of poor property accountability. Cases of willful neglect should be dealt with, however, the first sergeant must be a key player to prevent Reports of Survey.

. . . adjust to the malassignment . . .

If you are fortunate enough to receive a bonafide 92Y supply sergeant with some years of experience who has grown up in a supply room and had the best of the old teachers, read no further. However, if you have a soldier who holds the position of supply sergeant and the system has not provided the opportunity for development, then you have your hands full. Again, do not assume that because the supply room looks orderly and neat that all is well. You can help with the supply sergeant's development. Taking no action means that a soldier someday will pay out of his or her pocket. One of the surest ways to check out your supply sergeant is to have the next higher headquarters come in to inspect. The inspector also should assess what the supply sergeant knows or does not know. Take recommendations on how to rectify the situation.

. . . what you need to know . . .

The first sergeant with no supply background knows enough about supply operations to be effective in developing the supply sergeant who might otherwise fail later, and in eradicating situations that cause Reports of Survey. You should take all the elementary courses dealing with unit supply that you can. Any course that contains information on property accountability should be completed when you assume your position. Require that the supply sergeant brief you on the state of the unit's supply operations. Because most of the hand-receipt holders are NCOs, require that the supply sergeant give the NCOs classes on supply accountability. The very first class should be titled, *Reports of Survey.*

The Importance of Property Accountability . . .

If you cannot find the time to take any of the elementary courses that would make you effective, take the best Army Regulations dealing with property accountability and study. Compose checklists and have some super supply sergeant that you know verify it for you.

Training NCO . . .

. . . must be the training doctrinal expert . . .

Ask yourself what is required to be a training NCO? What should the training NCO read prior to the appointed duty? How can the first sergeant check to ensure that he or she did the directed reading?

The following are minimum required reading for a training NCO:

◊ FM 25-2, Unit Training Management
◊ AR 614-200, Selection of Enlisted Soldiers for Training and Assignment
◊ AR 600-200, Chap. 7, Enlisted Personnel Management System
◊ FM 25-100, FM 25-101
◊ AR 350-series and MACOM 350-series Regulations and Supplements
◊ Higher headquarters directives, training notes, and guidance.

The training NCO must be able to answer the following questions for the leadership groups:

How is the unit's training information for the training meeting verified?

1. What is the primary purpose of the time-management system?
2. What role does the "Long-Range" Planning Calendar play in the long-range plan?
3. What is training strategy?
4. Define training terms:

◊ Battlefield Operating System, battle focus, battle task, principles of training, pre-execution checks, precombat checks.

5. Why is risk assessment important?

6. How does the training NCO receive the Family Support Agenda information from family members?

7. Why are drafted copies of the training schedules important?

Dining Facility Manager . . .

Focus on those duties and responsibilities that the dining facility manager must ensure to make the command, the unit, and the facility manager successful. The first sergeant should not try to learn the job of the dining facility manager or even control the facility.

The critical tasks of the dining facility manager in both garrison and field environments are what the first sergeant needs to understand. What does the first sergeant need to know to check the checker? What does the first sergeant need to know to feel comfortable with dining facility operation?

The task list to come is by no means all-inclusive and we advise that the list be used as a manager's tool by subtracting certain common-sense items on the list and adding after-the-fact important items picked up in discussions with the dining facility manager, we developed the following list of tasks a first sergeant should understand:

1. Is the headcounter in the grade of E4 or above?

2. Is there a detailed headcount SOP on hand with sample forms and necessary instruction forms attached (DA Form 3033, DA Form 1544, DA Form 3032)?

3. Is the dining facility officer designated on DA Form 1687 and a memorandum on file in the dining facility to receive and sign for DD Form 1544 books?

4. Is DD Form 1544 (cash sheets) signed prior to issue to the dining facility, with complete heading to include meal rates and surcharge?

5. Were all the DD form 1544 (cash collections sheet) that were used, together with money turned in to the dining facility officer, turned in to finance? Is a copy of DD Form 1131 on file (before cash collection came to a total of $500 and once at the end of the month)?

6. Are DA Forms 3546-R (Control Record for Dining Facility) used to issue all sheets to the headcount, and are all used forms on file?

7. Are there two safes or other identifiable locations for cash meal payment books (one in the dining facility, one for dining facility officer)?

8. Are there DD Forms 1687 (Notice of Delegation of Authority—Receipt of Supplies) on hand to authorize the receipt of supplies (Class 1)?

9. Are there DA Forms 2970 (Ration Request/Feeder Report) provided to the dining facility from the PAC on a daily basis?

10. Are memoranda in the dining facility files to support all Class I subsistence consumed outside the dining facility?

11. Are all MREs and FPAs maintained for individual package on DA Form 5309-R on file in the dining facility? FPA (Food Packet Assault).

12. Is the dining facility account within three (3) percent (+ or -) each month and at zero or underdrawn at the end of the fiscal year (DD Form 3980-R, Dining Facility Account Card)?

13. Are DA Forms 3988-R, Dining Facility Equipment Replacement, maintained and verified by the Food Service Adviser on file?

14. Are there job books and OJT training files IAW FM 10-23 on file in the dining facility? Some of the information that should be contained in these files are school quotas, SDT scores, PT and weapons scores, height and weight data, counseling statements (good and bad), boards (cook of quarter), promotion information concerning the soldier, soldier of the month, etc.

15. Are required publications on hand?

16. Is hot food maintained at holding temperature of 140°F (60°C) or above? Is the cold food maintained at 45°F (7°C) or below IAW TB MED 530?

17. Is food in walk-in refrigeration and storage rooms stored six inches above the floor? Is the food in reach labeled, marked, or stamped with date/time IAW TB MED 530?

18. Are supervisors inspecting daily all personnel who work in the dining facility at the start of their work period? Are personnel who exhibit signs of illness being referred to the installation Medical Authority (IMA)?

19. With the exception of plain wedding bands, are supervisors enforcing the rule that personnel will not wear jewelry such as braceletes, watches, or other similar items?

20. Are personnel who handle or serve food being used to clean latrines, garbage cans, sewage, or perform similar custodial duties during work periods?

21. Are signs conspicuously posted directing all personnel to wash their hands after using the toilet or using tobacco?
22. Are the meal hours/serving periods adequate (90 minutes are required/normal serving times)? Serving/eating times (hours) will be based on:

    a. number of diners
    b. size and type of facility
    c. work or training schedule
    d. distance between the facility and duty station

The above questions mainly concern the garrison-type dining facility operation. The following concern field-type dining facility operation. You should know enough about these operations to monitor and evaluate, but your purpose is not to manage.

1. Has enough lead time for ration requests been allowed for Class I (Ration) support (30 day minimum)?
   NOTE: Normally two hot meals are fed as breakfast and dinner meals with an operational meal (MRE) for lunch.
2. Is there an established menu for the ration cycle, for example, A-Ration, T-Ration, or B-Rations, A-MRE-A, T-MRE-A, B-MRE-T, B-MRE-B, etc. May rations may be mixed?
3. Have enhancements been requested and programmed for issue (fresh fruits, cereal, and mandatory milk, bread, and condiments)? Have additional warm and cool beverages been considered, ordered, funded?
4. Has a need for potable ice, water, gas, and landfill (location) been identified?
5. Do all the cooks have operators identification cards for the M-S Burner units, gasoline lanterns, immersion heaters, or the generator?
6. Will the unit be using paper products/flatware or mess kits? If paper products/flatware is to be used, have the items in correct amounts been requested through supply (SSSC)?
7. Has all the equipment been operationally checked and is there a workable loading plan?
8. Is the dining facility within the 3% tolerance on the over and under record, DA Form 3251-R?

9. Is there a workable field SOP addressing some of the issues contained in these questions?
10. Are insulated food containers chilled for cold and pre-heated for hot food?
11. Does the field SOP contain a picture of the suggested layout for a field kitchen site from FM 10-23?
12. Are required publications on hand or order? The following are some of those publications:

   a. AR 15-6, Procedures for Investigating Officers and Board of Officers.
   b. AR 40-15, Nutrition Allowances, Standards, and Education
   c. AR 600-38, Meal Card Management System
   d. AR 30-16, Food Service Data Feedback Program
   e. CTA 50-909, Field and Garrison Furnishings and Equipment
   f. FM 10-23-1, Commander's Guide to Food Service Operations
   g. FM 10-23, Army Food Service Operations
   h. DA PAM 25-400-2, Modern Army Record Keeping System
   i. SB 10-495, Standard "B" Ration for the Armed Forces

The tasks of training, administration, maintenance, assessment, and upkeep of the soldiers' organizational life demand the full participation of every concerned leader in the unit.

Interactor Stage #2 . . .

Functions of the Management

◊ Ensure the functions of leadership
◊ Ensure the functions of systems
◊ Ensure the functions of equal opportunity
◊ Ensure the functions of discipline
◊ Ensure the functions of nonpunitive disciplinary measures
◊ Ensure the function of administrative personnel actions
◊ Ensure the functions of healthy lifestyle
◊ Ensure the functions of the Armed Forces Disciplinary Control Board
◊ Ensure the functions of the Family Advocacy Program

THE DIAMOND, SECOND EDITION

◊ Ensure the functions that ensure trainers are trained to train
◊ Ensure the functions of the multi-echelon training engineer

Section XI:

The First Sergeant's Intent . . .

Numerous Army publications explain the commander's intent and how the command is to apply that intent. We would like to introduce what is to be hereafter called, "The First Sergeant's Intent." This introduction is necessary to emphasize that you, first sergeant, cannot drop the glass balls while you are present for duty, and you cannot allow the glass balls to be dropped when you are absent.

. . . of human stuff . . .

Diamond wearers are soldiers too, just as human as the rest of unit leadership. For these and other reasons, during the first sergeant's tour of duty, he or she cannot be expected to go year in and year out without being absent. When they go, does the unit just shut down? Are those decisions normally made by the first sergeant to be put on hold until his or her return? Are operations supporting the soldier's organizational life that the first sergeant juggles so well to be put on the "back burner?" If in fact any of the above happens, the first sergeant has failed. A first sergeant who feels so insecure that he or she does not allow another soldier in the unit to make decisions in his or her absence should not be in that position. The position itself requires that you (first sergeant) train soldiers to replace you.

Next Qualified Leader . . .

. . . ready to do the job . . .

Therefore, we introduce the "first sergeant's intent." The next qualified leader who steps forward in the first sergeant's absence need not go through a training/learning process to figure out which balls are in the air and which cannot hit the ground. This qualified leader needs to have a high degree of confidence that all systems will remain in a-go-status. This leader should take the first sergeant's well-planned schedule of events, those frameworks of leadership, and continue to affect situations at the levels maintained by the first sergeant. The leader is not necessarily the next ranking leader, but instead the next qualified leader.

This qualified leader will not be a clone of the first sergeant but will know the first sergeant's goals and will conduct business in a manner that fits your frameworks of leadership.

This qualified replacement for the first sergeant, in his or her absence or unceremonial dismissal, should know that only inactivity guarantees error-free performance, and that fear of failure must not become terror.

Section X:

Duties Promoter . . .

Healthy Lifestyle Behaviors:

◊ Physical conditioning
◊ Weight control
◊ Substance abuse
◊ Nutrition
◊ Stress management
◊ Anti-tobacco
◊ Dental health

Health and physical fitness encompasses the nutritional, physical, and mental fitness of soldiers. Promote fitness, not because an Army regulation requires it, but because the first sergeant cares for the health and well-being of the unit's soldiers and their families.

Health Social Interaction:

◊ With the soldiers
◊ With the staff
◊ With the military-civilian population
◊ With the family members

Diamond Point: The first sergeant as the multi-echelon social engineer projects health social aspects into the organization life.

Diamond Point: The first sergeant's follow-on supervising and support tasks (FSSTs) requires that the diamond wearer assures total unit involvement.

Duties: Juggler . . .

* Training
  ◊ Marksmanship
  ◊ NBC
  ◊ Establish Top Five Quarterly Priorities

  ◊ Training Brief

  ◊ Junior Officers
  ◊ Junior NCOs

* Assessments
  ◊ Marksmanship
  ◊ NCOER
  ◊ Uniform wear

  ◊ Training
  ◊ Social-psychological involvement
  ◊ NBC
  ◊ PMCS

* Communications
  ◊ internal
  ◊ external

* Administration
  ◊ Training
  ◊ Systems Design
  ◊ Priority Processing

  ◊ Athletics
  ◊ Supply
  ◊ Discipline

* Inspections:
  ◊ Barracks
  ◊ Soldiers/Troops
  ◊ Work Areas
  ◊ TA 50

  ◊ Records
  ◊ DA Form 2166-8-1s
  ◊ Equipment

* Public Relations with:
  ◊ AFDCB
  ◊ Post Agencies
  ◊ Off-Post Establishments (AR 190-24)
  ◊ Family Support Groups

* Analyzer
  ◊ Climate
  ◊ Organizational Life
  ◊ Training

* Maintenance
  ◊ Vehicles
  ◊ Weapons
  ◊ Equipment

* Implementor
  ◊ Creating Command Climate
  ◊ Tapping soldier potential
  ◊ Developing leaders

Diamond Point: The first sergeant always ensures that both the objective and subjective combat effectiveness indicators are included in all of the above duties.

... able to perform ...

Therefore, if the first sergeant has done his or her job well, a qualified leader will be produced who understands that he or she has enough freedom to perform at peak levels without substituting his or her own goals for those that have been clearly established by the first sergeant. It is the first sergeant's desire to free the positive, productive potential while achieving the unit's goals and protecting performance standards.

... carry the mission on ...

Senior NCOs need to grasp this first sergeant's intent in order to ensure that because the first sergeant is absent for an extended period of time, the bottom does not fall out of the company operations. Soldier programs, boarding soldier, checks required before the soldier is presented to the external world (the world outside of normal unit), barracks standards, BTRs, chapter actions, Article 15s, soldier problems (counseling center), and all of those things that comprise the first sergeant's implied, specified, and directed duties must be maintained at the same high standards, as if the first sergeant was still present for duty.

Test the Intent ...

The first sergeant's intent needs to be exercised before the diamond wearer is absent from the unit. The best way to accomplish this task is to first identify the qualified leader who would replace you in the event of your absence. The second step is to give this leader regulatory guidance, and at every opportunity train and explain your critical duties. The third step is conducting the practical exercise while you are around to make adjustments. The fourth and last step is to require the selected leader to read your copy of "The Diamond."

... must understand commander duty connection ...

Your selected replacement must also understand that many of the specified duties of the commander are transformed into implied duties for the first sergeant. Above all, your replacement should realize that in your absence, he or she is the first sergeant. There is no such thing as the "acting" first sergeant. This is why everyone must understand the "first sergeant's intent." Your replacement is only acting when he or she fails to perform in carrying out the "first sergeant's intent."

The senior most qualified is not required to step into the job the first day knowing all that there is to know about the duties and tasks of the position. The idea of understanding the "first sergeant intent" is to drastically reduce the orientation period experienced by an individual assuming a new position. The very first day must be a clear, step-by-step agenda of required activities. The practice of activating this agenda must be done many times before there is a requirement to execute.

Principles of the first sergeant intent:

Principle #1—There is no such thing as an acting first sergeant. In the absence of the first sergeant, the selected replacement is expected to carry out all the first sergeant duties and tasks.

Principle #2—All must understand that many of the specified duties of the commander are automatically transformed into implied duties for the first sergeant.

Principle #3—The first sergeant's intent requires an exercise to be totally successful, following the steps as outlined in the section of intent.

Principle #4—The absence of the first sergeant is not an excuse for suspending the duties and tasks of the position. Only inactivity guarantees error-free performance.

Principle #5—The first sergeant must not feel so insecure that he or she fails to train a qualified replacement.

Principle #6—Exercising the intent also requires agenda activation, which is an idea that is supported by the frameworks for leadership and the chronological milestone.

Intent and Duties Connection . . .

The outline is intended to point out that in most cases, the specified duties of the commander can be transformed into implied duties for the first sergeant. While a failure would belong to the commander, the first sergeant would share that failure. This also implies that in the absence of the commander, the first sergeant should carry out his or her doing tasks. First sergeant, because you are of "human stuff" and will have to be absent at some point in time, and you support the commander's specified duties, it is important that your replacement have knowledge of your duties. It is even more important that your replacement understand the commander's specified / first sergeant implied duties relationship.

Training . . .
Improve Warfighting Capability Principal Trainer . . .

The diamond wearer is the unit's principal trainer. The diamond wearer knows all there is to know about training. What you know must include managing, policy-making, objectives, and training programs. The task does not stop with just knowing about training, but extends to being able to articulate to even the most junior-leader those standards that you will enforce and require complete knowledge of.

NCO's Critical Tasks . . .

. . . a trained trainer . . .
Critical tasks training (CTT) for NCOs must be your principal focus. Once it has been established that NCOs know the importance of training, your key task then is to ensure that the trainer is trained. If the first sergeant fail to ensure that the trainer is trained, he or she will find his or herself micro-managing training more than the first sergeant should. You will be confident that all of your unit's training is always ready for anyone's inspection. Junior leaders will tell you that they understand the fundamentals of training, that their goal is to teach a soldier something new or improve on what was taught. However, until you are shown what they know, then assume they do not know. You must develop with your NCO Corps a commitment to training. You must clearly identify and mandate the standards that will produce a force ready to deploy, to fight, and to win, as well as a family support system to back it all up.

Diamond Point: Stratify your framework for training the unit's leadership groups. Time is wasted in planning and training senior NCOs in the same tasks as those taught to junior NCOs.

Translating Fundamentals:

NCOs should be able to recite and translate the fundamentals of training that will produce effectiveness. Understanding the fundamentals of good order and discipline as a command responsibility is not enough; that understanding must be translated into high morale and wise leadership by NCOs as the most effective means of attaining and sustaining good order and discipline.

Dereliction in Training . . .

Dereliction in training is a most serious matter that should concern leaders at all levels. If NCOs fail to understand their dereliction, they fail in their responsibility to the most noblest creature on the face of this Earth . . . the American soldier. Taking care of our soldiers is a sacred trust for the military professional. You, first sergeant, must insist that your soldiers understand that they are at the point of a bayonet when they train. War does not allow us time to get ready.

Dereliction in training is when you allow one or more of the below listed conditions to exist:

1. Training in your unit is given a priority other than priority one. Training is given lip service. Training is not viewed as a way of life.
2. Command climates exist that are not conducive to individual development.
3. Prescribed conditions of the training develop that are not the standards required.
4. Failure is apparent to consider proficiency levels and skill decay, and to build in sustainment.
5. Failure is evident to reach out for the great challenges and opportunities in training our soldiers.
6. NCOs are unable to recite or translate the fundamentals of training.

Training that builds on maintaining and emphasizing the importance of day-to-day training readiness supports warfighting capability. Training readiness is conceived, taught, ingested, and digested by the leadership of your unit only when all truly believe that you are "Mr. Training."

It is wise that you as well as your subordinate leaders study the tenet of failure for the purpose of prevention. Junior leaders will make mistakes because of errors in judgment or lack of experience and knowledge. These types of errors are not dereliction but learning.

Training . . .

In training, you are attempting to acclimate soldiers to the realities of the field in war. The most common experience in training is to witness soldiers doing things wrong, or worse, doing nothing. You have to stop thinking of training in its simplest form but put it in its new, broader and more complex context to meet the challenges of this new technological field of war.

Diamond Point: If the first sergeant fail in his or her attempt to acclimate soldiers to the realities of war, they will fail the test on the field of battle.

. . . if it is important to the first sergeant, it will be important to junior leaders . . .

The new objective of training is to cause subordinate leaders to willingly accept specified training goals as their own and to work wholeheartedly for the achievement of those goals. However, first sergeant, it is you, the senior enlisted soldier, who is ultimately responsible for translating that understanding of importance into appropriate training techniques. It is important to the subordinate leaders if it is important to their soldiers' survivorship and if it is important to the first sergeant. Once the subordinate leaders willingly accept specified training goals as their own, they must be monitored so they cannot downgrade or alter training without the first sergeant's knowledge.

. . . First Sergeant's involvement a must . . .

Then the key to successful training hinges simply on the first sergeant's interaction with the subordinate leadership. It does not matter how good the training of NCOs is, training is a success only when the first sergeant chairs the training meeting. The first sergeant must be a hard disciplinarian concerning the planning, assessment, execution, reassessment, and after-action review to keep the focus on warfighting. Successful training does not allow any operating section in the unit to continue its day-to-day mission during training periods.

Interlocking Training Systems . . .

The attainment and sustainment of marksmanship skill is the commander's intent when soldiers go to the range to fire their individually assigned weapons. With your sights set on firing the weapon, do not lose the many training opportunities on and off the range.

The unit may not be able to march the soldiers all the way to the range, however, the unit can have them dismount six miles from the range and fast march in tactically, practicing a few tactical maneuvers along the way, such as taking up a defense position and simulated nuclear, biological, and chemical attack responses. Once the soldiers arrive at the range, treat the location as a base camp about to be attacked by the enemy. Everything should be done tactically, i.e., feeding, patrolling, crew serve NBC equipment, MOPP training, etc.

Diamond Point: Foot marches should be done IAW Field Manual No. 21-18 (Foot Marches).

Once the soldiers move up to fire, the unit cannot always be hung up on qualification without practice. Use the range for practice, as well as for qualification. Practice and practice lying in wait for the enemy in foul and fair weather, night or day. And as the soldier lies awaiting, simulate the enemy attack by having targets pop up (not in all lanes and not all at once). This is part of the psychological training that soldiers must experience in training to prepare for war.

Subordinate leaders must learn to lead tactical scenarios that enhance the attainment and sustainment objective. These junior leaders must ask what are trained soldiers saying about the quality of training? Why is the word "boring" often associated with training?

Diamond Point: Ensure that all the unit NCOs understand that war is "come as you are." The cost of untrained/unpreparedness is lives and defeat.
Diamond Point: The first sergeant uses all of the skills and knowledge acquired over the years to ensure that the program of training incorporates all of the intricacies that will ensure soldier's servivability (battlefield requirements).

Section XII: TRAINING MANAGEMENT
TRAINING ASSESSMENT

The first sergeant's doing tasks (DTs) . . .

The diamond wearer must first of all ensure that all subordinate leaders understand the importance of assessment which actually starts when the training is planned. The analysis of the training information provided through assessment is the key mechanism that all leadership groups use in the formation of future individual soldier critical tasks training.

Same as with training execution, the wearer ensures that the unit's training time incorporate these management tools to determine how well the training is or was executed to Army standards.

It is the diamond wearer who verifies and certifies that the noncommissioned officer conducting the training is highly qualified to enhance the training experience for the evaluated unit by providing valid, credible observations.

The wearer is most concerned with the assessment of training proficiency on mission essential task list tasks, especially the "Ps" (needs practice) or "Us" (untrained).

The first sergeant's direct supervising and supporting tasks (DSSTs) are focused on the following:

- The process that allows training participants to discover for themselves what happened, why it happened, and how it can be done better. This is mainly done by having the junior leaders review and comment on the assessment.
- Require that the junior leader incorporate a training assessor, annotating the designated assessor on the series of rough draft training schedules.
- Directing that the assessment discussions be methods of improving the planning and execution of training. Junior leaders must leave these discussions with new knowledge and attitudes about critical tasks training.
- Provide quality advice and recommendations that could involve external sources.
- Recommend bullet comments (NCOER) for noncommissioned officer who produce quality training (interjecting new ideas and methods).

TRAINING PLANNING

The first sergeant's doing tasks (DTs) . . .

The first sergeant chief doing task in the training planning phase is to involve all the leadership groups in looking at what happened in the training execution and evaluation; and deciding what training tasks need to be executed in the short-range and the long-range future. The diamond wearer knows that the failure to consider how training was executed and what were the results according to the evaluation really voids the whole training management process. Much of the planning must be based on what was done and what was not done to reach the objectives so stated in the mission essential tasks. Did the training in fact reach a fully or partial trained level? That is the question that must be answered by all unit leaders.

The first sergeant's doing tasks regarding training planning for the unit are designed to support training planning rather than having the first sergeant and the training noncommissioned officer taking the planning lead, creating a responsibility void. The first sergeant should continuously stress that long-range and short-range planning design is to be checked and re-checked until the training becomes near-term training.

Another first sergeant's doing tasks that must be considered in training planning is the knowledge of the combat effectiveness indicators (both subjective and objective indicators). These factors will influence the outcome of unit training, therefore, should never be overlooked in the training cycle.

The first sergeant's direct supervising and supporting tasks (DSSTs) for training planning is mainly focused on the following:

- Ensuring the training planners (different leadership groups involved) are not confused about what training should be included in the long-range and the training that should be included in short-range. The first sergeant therefore monitors the understanding of the rationale for inclusion.
- Ensures that the training noncommissioned officer produce the required number of rough draft training schedules. This provides the first sergeant the tool to analyze junior leader's planning skills.
- Tracks the training cycle and ensure that planning is in according to its required design.

TRAINING EXECUTION

The first sergeant's doing tasks (DTs) . . .

The diamond wearer must ensure that in planning for the training execution, the unit's training schedule(s) must allow for detailed inspections and checks to be performed prior to the execution and that the time be allowed for those specific purposes. The schedules must contain time that reflects that prerequisite training is to be conducted (allows the training concentration to be on the main critical tasks).

It is the diamond wearer's focus on the overall unit's training status that allows the wearer to know that the unit's leaders are trained and prepared to train.

Most important of all, it is doing the conduct of the training meeting that the diamond wearer's doing tasks are put into play. For example, a leader whose preliminary training plan does not have the right focus or who has tried to schedule too many tasks, the wearer interjects the Army standards as well as recommendations. It is during the training meeting that the wearer projects out the number of soldiers who will be present for training and the number that will be absent for legitimate reasons, i.e., projected sick call, leaves, charge of quarters, confinements, court-martials, etc.

The first sergeant's chief doing tasks is to ensure that the unit's training is executed according to near-term planning and that distractions are held to a minimum. The first sergeant also makes notes and monitors the skills, attitudes and display of knowledge of the noncommissioned officers.

The first sergeant's direct supervising and supporting tasks (DSSTs) . . .

To sum up the wearer's requirement to complete these tasks is to ensure that all subordinate leaders understand that the proper execution of training to standard is a difficult but rewarding process. The key word is preparation (prerequisite and preliminary). The wearer's main focus in the performance of these tasks is to ensure that the subordinate leaders perform their doing tasks (DTs) and direct supervising and supporting tasks (DSSTs) to Army standards.

. . . training management . . .

Determining the direct supervising and supporting tasks (DSSTs) for the diamond wearer concerning training must first be provide training answers to be able to understand the training direction. The questions are:

◊ Why does assessment begin the training planning process?
Note: This question must be broken down to the lowest terms for the junior leaders.

◊ Since the commander relies on junior leader's feedback to determine their unit's training proficiency level, whose responsibility is it to verify the quality of junior leader's feedback?

◊ How does the diamond wearer react to the following two results of in-depth assessment . . .
. . . demonstrated strengths?
. . . need to improve training proficiency on specific weaknesses?

◊ Who is directly responsible for the unit's training strategy for collective mission essential tasks?

◊ Who is directly responsible for the unit's training strategies for individual and leader tasks (those that support collective mission essential tasks)?

◊ What is the three dimension line of thinking with regards to training?

. . . translating the commander's analysis . . .

As the commander completes the analysis of the assessment that identifies training strengths and weaknesses, the contents of the analysis is presented to the first sergeant who translates this information to the leadership groups directly affected. The most often and best method used is the unit training meeting. Most of what is discussed, directed, implied, etc. must be heard by all leaders who attend the training meetings. Training meetings contain a wealth of professional development information for junior leaders. The knowledge of the identified training strengths and weaknesses by the junior leader (direct trainer) is analyzed to determine what leadership skills need to be applied.

The junior leader's knowledge of what requires a training strategy and the skill to realign the mission's essential tasks must be verified by the first sergeant. The knowledge also includes the intricacies of the tasks (the subtasks, the key points of the tasks, only obtained from training experience). It is often these intricacies of a task that mean the difference between quality training and training that is assessed as substandard.

Key points, factors and actions or reactions that present the soldiers with interesting, realistic and challenging training situations is the body of these intricacies. The training strategy focuses on training deficiencies which impact on the unit's ability to perform its wartime mission (selected essential leader and soldier tasks must also be integrated into collective mission essential tasks). The first sergeant welds the noncommissioned officer's knowledge of the tasks' intricacies to the training strategy thereby sustaining, maintaining, refreshing a comprehensive strategy; to train all supporting tasks not executed to standard.

Diamond Point: The diamond wearer maintains direct contact with the noncommissioned officer(s) who is required to prepare a comprehensive strategy to ensure that all the intricacies are considered. Preparing a comprehensive training strategy is in itself a training tool for junior leaders. Therefore, the diamond wearer establishes a monitoring position of the planning activities, interjecting information when required.

It is that comprehensive training strategy backed by knowledge and skill that gives the quarterly training brief (AC) (QTB) or yearly training brief (RC) (YTB) the validity that the untrained ("U") METL tasks will be trained to standard. The training strategy brief (YTB) crosses the ear of those who will evaluate it to determine if it meets the tough, realistic, or safety requirement. The first sergeant, then, is the unit's critical element who ensures that the members at the training meeting don't overlook critical ingrediences. The first sergeant then considers the impact of new personnel, new equipment, resources allocation, multi-echelon training, etc. as the training schedules take form.

The first sergeant's doing tasks (DTS) demands that the diamond wearer conducts a timely, well-structured, well-organized, and recurring training meeting focused only on "T" (trained), "P" (need practice) and "U" (untrained) tasks. In other words, focused on training issues only (the who, where, when, what, how, why, what-if, quantities, etc.).

Training Meeting:

The first sergeant understands that there are "pre-training meeting considerations and actions" to ensure that all the real issues that need to be discussed are given some thought prior to the meeting. Also the fact that advance information needs to be disseminated to all the attendees.

Included in the advance notices that the diamond wearer must communicate to the junior leaders is the current up-to-date training guidance from higher commanders. Considerations include but are not limited to:

◊ multiechelon training opportunities
◊ leader(s) designated to provide feedback for assessment of up-coming training
◊ problems or distracters to identify and overcome
◊ training oriented on the METL tasks
◊ safety integrated into training, training integrated into safety
◊ the content of the series of draft training schedules

Diamond Point: A first sergeant's teaching point for the unit's noncommissioned officers is that a meeting (having a known place, time, and subjects to be discussed) should be given advance thought. The attending NCOs should be ready to provide quality and constructive data that will answer the who, where, when, what, how, why, what-if, quantities, etc.

Diamond Point: The first sergeant clarifies for the leadership groups the difference between the commander's training strategy and the strategy the NCOs are required to develop using the three dimension line of thinking (mainly concerned with individual soldier tasks).

Diamond Point: The first sergeant ensures that the training meetings are included on the series of rough drafted training schedules.

The first sergeant directs the training meeting's line of thinking in three dimensions (long-range, short-range, and near-term). All three dimensions directly or indirectly impact the training schedules. At every training meeting there should be a series of draft training schedules (the unit's primary management tool is to ensure training is conducted on time and by qualified trainers with the necessary resources.) The series of draft training schedules reflect the three dimension concept.

The direct supervising and supporting tasks (DSSTs) for the diamond wearer concerning training meeting(s) is to instill procedures and methods in the minds of the subordinate leaders by setting the standards before, during, and after the meetings. These procedures are to be applied whether the first sergeant is present or elsewhere performing another equally important task. The unit's training meeting is where the "how" and the "why" of the trained (T), needs practice (P), and the untrained (U) is bashed out before it is put on the table at the higher headquarters. Therefore the diamond wearer institute consistent mechanisms to ensure that the unit's training meetings achieve their objectives.

The diamond wearer, through unit designed communication media, provides the junior leaders with the contents of the commander's analysis of METL training. These internal advance notices allow the junior leaders to prepare details for the training strategy to be presented at the next training meeting and eventually a training brief.

The diamond wearer helps provide all the necessary input for the junior leader who finds it difficult to develop a tough, realistic, and safe training strategy. However, it is the junior leader who prepares the training strategy.

Diamond Point: The first sergeant takes note of the state of preparedness of the junior leaders. How well did the junior leaders use the advance information to prepare? Here is the opportunity to develop a few bullet comments concerning a leader's preparedness.

It is the first sergeant's established relationship with the leadership groups that give the unit noncommissioned officer corps its substance. The requirement for a comprehensive training strategy for supporting tasks not executed to standards, most of the time, does not come from any one single individual or group. Synergistic forces are in a constant state of generating the power of the corps. The diamond wearer knows that the best quality for a training strategy will come from the input (knowledge and skills) of as many NCOs as possible. This is another way that the diamond wearer supports the leader's over-all professional competency.

The diamond wearer notes the degree of input from each member attending the training meeting; that the input shows that effort was made on the part of the concerned leaders. The inception of a training strategy by a platoon sergeant may require the diamond wearer's in-depth experience (of which the wearer offers freely). This involvement represents the diamond wearer's exercise of the direct supervising and supporting tasks (DSSTs). Likewise, if the inception of a training strategy becomes a stumbling block for a squad leader, the diamond wearer is just as committed to the squad leader accomplishing the training strategy mission as with the platoon sergeant. However, the wearer's involvement is the exercise of the follow-on supervising and support tasks (FSSTs). The best way to keep the assignment of the tasks in perspective is to think of the chain—the next level down under the diamond wearer use the DSSTs and if the wearer interacts in any way with leaders below the DSSTs, it is then FSSTs.

The first sergeant checks for proper preparation of training not only for the confidence it gives the trainer but to ensure that leaders are performing their required tasks to standards. The platoon sergeant performs direct supervising and supporting tasks (DSSTs) by ensuring that the squad leader(s) rehearse their preparations and review the tasks and subtasks to be covered during their training. If the platoon sergeant is the principle trainer, then the first sergeant performs direct supervising and supporting tasks (DSSTs) by ensuring that the platoon sergeant(s) rehearse their preparations and review the tasks and subtasks to be trained.

Diamond Point: The senior leader assesses their junior leader's competencies and provides developmental feedback when performing DSSTs and FSSTs.

There are several tasks (actions) that must be accomplished by the senior leaders to ensure that all the trainers are prepared to present their training. These actions, i.e., identify weak points in the training plan, use of effective training techniques, giving them confidence in their ability to train, etc. incorporating the first sergeant's doing tasks (DT) to monitor the training prep activities. The first sergeant is mindful that for training to meet the required standards, these activities must be or become training habit.

... the command sergeant major's role in unit training management...

The first sergeant maintains that the role of the command sergeant major in unit training management is an indirect role because of the fact that standing between the CSM and the unit's training is a commander and a first sergeant. The commander and first sergeant's position and management techniques must be respected. If the command sergeant major takes up a role other than an indirect role, conflict is inevitable. The unit level command team is directly responsible for that unit's training (individual and collective). All others who could become involved in training management take on an indirect role at unit level.

The command sergeant major's indirect training management role is based on years of training experience to monitor, evaluate, report, recommend, advise, analyze and to provide the commanders with extracted training performance data to be used in the analysis of the organization's mission essential tasks. Therefore, the CSM must never be given a specified or directed task in training management that would cause direct conflict with the unit level command team(s).

However, the unit level command teams must understand that the command sergeant major must be allowed to carry out indirect duties and responsibilities concerning training management if the CSM is to provide the organization commander with credible data for training analysis.

Diamond Point: The diamond wearer maintains a synergistic unit training philosophy.

... follow-on supervising and support tasks (FSSTs) ...

The follow-on supervising and support tasks (FSSTs) for the diamond wearer are as important for the diamond wearer as they are for any enlisted leader. However, for the diamond wearer, the performance of these tasks take on a greater significance than for any other enlisted leader. The main reason for this greater significance is that one of the diamond wearer's direct supervising and supporting tasks (DSSTs) is to ensure that the performance of this task is first understood by all junior leaders and secondly that this task is performed by the platoon level leaders.

Therefore, the first sergeant understands that in order to perform these important leadership tasks to the standards that support the operational, functional, social, etc. requirements of the unit, all subordinate leaders must understand the design of the follow-on supervising and support tasks. It is important that junior leaders understand the design for their future development and to understand what the first sergeant is doing when performing these tasks. The performing of these tasks by the first sergeant directly impact into the performance of every junior leader in the unit.

The first sergeant understands that by performing these tasks that it is a technique of looking several leadership levels down the leadership chain to determine how well the junior levels are performing and to direct or conduct adjustment(s) as required.

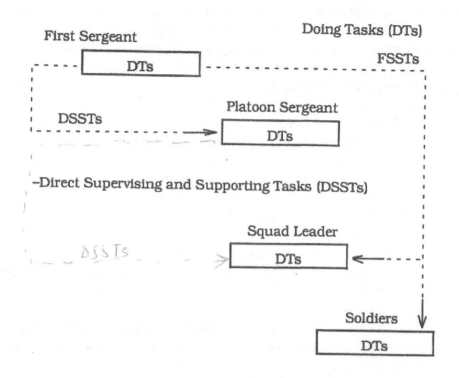

—This figure shows the leadership and tasks relationship—

When performing these tasks (FSSTs), the first sergeant is directly evaluating the squad leader while indirectly evaluating the platoon sergeant's performance. In other words, how does the first sergeant determine the platoon sergeant's effectiveness and developmental impact on their platoons?

Section XIII

Speech Making:

Position design dictates that first sergeants be required to make speeches in front of people and organizations (military and civilian).

Eloquence in speaking comes with practice, study and watching the techniques of the speakers the first sergeants hears and observes through their developmental years. Eloquence is important in itself as another factor to get the message across, the main purpose of any speech should be to get a message of importance to the audience. Quality speeches still require practice, study, and watching those who make speeches.

Some of the questions that the enlightened diamond wearer ask concerning speech making are:

◊ Will I ever be in a position where I will have to make a speech or present a proposal to a group or an organization?
◊ What do I need to do over the years to help me prepare myself for the day I will be called upon to present a speech?
◊ Where can I find information for the study of speech making?
◊ With whom can I speak in my quest to develop myself for the task?
◊ Will I ever overcome my feeling of fear of speech making?
◊ What can I do when I am alone to practice the art of speech making?

The enlightened first sergeant develops a program of learning to ensure that this important task is accomplished to personal standards. The program can be as simple as the following:

• Develop three to five minute speeches on certain topics and practice recitation when convenient.

Note: Don't throw these practice speeches away, establish a speech file (to be worked and improved on as you grow with military life).

As you practice your speech, raise and lower your voice (inflection). It should be natural, not forced. Speak as clearly as possible. Concentrate on pronouncing or accenting each syllable distinctly and correctly.

Pauses are to speaking what punctuation is to writing. Pause during your speaking, sometimes to take a breath; sometimes for effect. The proper use of pauses allows the audience to absorb ideas and take notes; allowing you to add emphasis, meaning and interpretation to what you are saying.

These are the diamond wearer's guidelines for speech making:

◊ Speak loud enough for all to hear without difficulty.
◊ Avoid a dull, boring monotone. Change the pitch of your voice for emphasis.

◊ Rate of speech should be governed by the thought, idea, or emotion you are trying to communicate.
◊ Solid preparation and rehearsal gives the confidence to overcome nervousness.
◊ Display a positive attitude.

The best advice is to just be natural. Let hands and arms hang freely. Don't wring or twist your hands. Shy away from the distracting mannerisms such as remaining glued to one spot or jiggling your pocket change. During rehearsal, have someone note any distracting mannerisms so that you can correct them.

The following is an example of a speech written from scratch by CSM Bobby Owens and presented at several noncommissioned officer's events:

"Leadership: What Is?"

Who must answer that question for you it is not I. Even though the field manuals (FMs) gives us a good solid definition of leadership and a path to follow—only you can answer the question, "Leadership: What Is?"

Notice that I didn't ask the question in the traditional style. From this point on—I want you to let ring in your mind "Leadership: What Is?" Every time you hear the word leadership or every time you look at those symbols of leadership that you wear—think of "Leadership: What Is?" Each time when you wake up in the morning before you touch anything—and I mean anything—think and ask the question—"Leadership: What Is?" Even when you think that you have a good definition of—"Leadership: What Is?" continue to ask. Each time you look down at your LES, before you raise your head, ask that question. Here right now, you should be asking yourself the question. "Leadership: What Is?"

If you fail to truly understand words like responsible, you will never get an answer to the question, "Leadership: What Is?"

Leadership requires that you to not only commit yourself to our Army, but it requires you to commit some other things and to commit far more than yourself. First of all you have to define for yourselves the word commitment as you define—"Leadership: What Is?" Leadership is not easy—It was never meant to be easy.

If you have not developed personal philosophies then you will find it hard to answer the question—"Leadership: What Is?" Some of these personal philosophies should sound like:

1) ALL soldiers below my grade belong to me.
2) Must know and understand what the Phantom's Philosophy is all about.
3) Always have a Plan "B" for mission success.
4) Study failure and its tenants.
5) Community life is everybody's business.
6) Work friendly: enjoy your job.
7) Seek a better way.

The definition as given in FM 22-100 (the old definition and the new one) is a very good definition and you need to focus on the old definition rather than the new one. You have to follow what is in the new FM 22-100 but the old definition is better.

The art of influence and directing soldiers in such a manner is to obtain their willing obedience, confidence, loyal respect and cooperation, in order to accomplish the mission. You have to break that down and dissect that for yourself—as I begin, I will not define it for you.

Understanding leadership is what the Noncommissioned Officer's Corps is all about. We have soldiers who retire and they never really understand the full value of what the Corps was all about. Why you ask, because no one ever asked them about the question, "Leadership: What Is?"

They will tell you all day that they have authority but cannot tell you from whence cometh that authority.

If you have difficulty differentiating the Military leadership from the type of leadership at Sears, you have a problem. If you don't understand why when the Sears work day is over, it's over. If you have never allowed your mind an explanation that explains if a Sears worker has a problem, family or financial—that worker has a problem. *Where as* there is no end to our Army leaders' work day. If our soldier has a problem, by the very nature of our work and the requirements of military leadership—that soldier's problem(s) becomes our problem. Our failure to understand this is what causes us to fail.

Leadership is an invisible strand as mysterious as it is powerful. It pulls unity out of disorder. Yet, it defies definition. No combination of talents can guarantee it. No process or training can create it where the spark does not exist.

The qualities of Leadership are universal: They are found in the poor and the rich, the humble and the proud, the common man, and the brilliant thinker; they are qualities that suggest paradox rather than pattern. But wherever they are found, Leadership—makes things happen.

Conclusion:

Judgement, initiative, decisiveness, courage and resourcefulness are all traits commonly found on the "laundry list" used to describe successful leaders. Leadership is all of these and more. It is the ability to rise above the mundane and to see beyond the narrow interests of an immediate world. It is the ability to lead those around you to share your vision, to share your commitment and to join us in our endeavors. It is the ability to understand people—their weaknesses. It is the strength never to compromise with truth. It is vitality and enthusiasm. There are no reluctant leaders.

Leadership is being able to say that you truly love people. That love of people is shown by thinking—"Leadership: What Is?"

CHAPTER VI

THE UNIFORM CODE OF MILITARY JUSTICE (AND THE NCO):

★ UCMJ: Faith in the Administrator
★ UCMJ: Questions NCO Must ask
★ Commander's Intent vs Congress' Intent
★ Terms of Military Justice
★ Knowledge of the System

    o   A Program of Learning

★ Points to Ponder
★ References
★ Disciplinary Infractions (Minor)

UCMJ: Faith in the Administrator . . .

If I had complete faith in human nature and a belief that all the commanders would perform their duties with consideration for soldiers, then I would not have written this section. If we all believed in the spirit of administering the law in accordance with the spirit of the United States Constitution, then I would be wasting your learning time with this information. All too often the UCMJ has been used as a tool to carry out the desires of a personal hidden agenda.

. . . administrator spirit vs the Constitution spirit . . .

What is written here is not meant to make you or your NCOs experts of the law. We want to leave development of that expertise to the Staff Judge Advocates Office. But you and your NCOs can help your soldiers understand the code and their rights. NCOs must possess enough knowledge of our justice system to ensure that the administrator's spirit is in fact in accordance with the spirit of our Constitution. Ignorance of the law is not only an excuse, it also means vacating the NCOs' responsibility to ensure the "sacred trust" to the noblest creature on the face of the Earth—the American soldier.

. . . actions will tell . . .

The actions of the administrator strengthen or can destroy faith in him or her. It does not require a keen analytical mind to conclude that the administrator is carrying out the desires of a personal hidden agenda. If this administrator does not display the guidance of AR 600-20, then you have to prepare for battle.

Diamond Point: Pointing out the administrator inconsistencies as you see them might be all that is required.

UCMJ: Questions Noncommissioned Officers Must Ask . . .

Answers must be found to questions concerning the procedures and prescribed policies governing the administration of military justice with regard to the unit's NCOs' involvement.

1. What are the procedures to get a soldier(s) expeditiously released from civilian confinement?

2. What are the command responsibilities to those soldiers in civilian confinement who cannot be expeditiously released?
3. What should be the required actions when improper command influence is identified?
4. What are the rules of escort to accompany the accused during trial?
5. What military justice terms should all NCOs be required to learn?
6. What are the general rules for soldiers selling personal property to other soldiers?
7. What are the general rules for the off-duty employment of soldiers?
8. What are the general rules for soldiers participating in political activities?
9. What are the general rules for soldiers accepting gratuities and soliciting gifts?
10. With whom must their requests for administrative hold be coordinated?
11. Why are administrative holds necessary?
12. What military publication explains the authority that an NCO should have?
13. What should be my action(s) when a soldier is not receiving due-process?

Diamond Point: Demand that unit NCOs start the thought process concerning military justice, using these questions as a starting point.

Commander's Intent vs Congress' Intent . . .

I have watched many soldiers who put their fate into the hands of commanders who had their own personal agendas when applying military criminal law. They had no intention of using published regulations to carry out the intent of Congress or ensure the basic rights of the soldier.

. . . enforcing the commander's enforcing of the law . . .

Because the commander has the specified duty of protecting the rights of soldiers and enforcing the law, these two duties fall into the implied category for the first sergeant. What does the first sergeant do when he realizes that the commander is carrying out the law in accordance with his or her own intent and not Congress' intent? Where does the loyalty of the first sergeant enter this picture? If the first sergeant accepts these false actions of the commander, he or she then becomes a part of this injustice.

The requirement for courage of the first sergeant will surface many times and this is one of those times when the first sergeant needs to step forward and state quite clearly that he or she will not be a part of any violation of basic rights. At the end of a tour of duty, the first sergeant should be able to say—I am proud of the military justice actions during my tour as first sergeant.

A Wedge . . .

. . . what do I do, what can I do? . . .

The action to be taken if the commander fails to understand his or her duties and responsibilities in the administration of military justice is simple. Discuss the case and your views, thoughts, and concerns with superiors, i.e., CSM, next higher commander. Secondly, build a file of memoranda to support your concerns. When the first sergeant have to build a file on the commander, something has gone wrong. I have always maintained that everyone who wears those tracks is not commander material.

The Words . . .

Never encourage a soldier to accept nonjudicial punishment when you know that "due process" to the commander is just words. Do not relay the horrors of a court martial when you know no consideration will be given to the soldier's guilt or the innocence if the soldier accepts the Article 15.

Exercising Military Authority . . .

NCOs have limits on how they are to exercise military authority. When, where, and how much military authority can NCOs exercise? What AR explains an NCO's military authority? The first sergeant must stress to your NCOs that before they can exercise military authority, they must know as much about military authority as possible.

. . . improving subject matter proficiency . . .

Learning about any subject that is foreign is resisted by the NCO Corps. The following are recommendations to improve the unit's NCO proficiency on the subject of military authority. The first sergeant's involvement is most definitely the key to programs of learning. Establish programs of learning to improve knowledge of all the support systems.

Diamond Point: Require as a matter of study the reading of NCO disciplinary policies in AR 600-20 . . .

. . . the authority to apprehend . . .

. . . to order into arrest or confinement . . .

. . . maintaining discipline in the Army . . .

. . . taking corrective action . . .

. . . NCO prerogatives and privileges.

Terms of Intent

Terms of Military Justice . . .

The program of learning (Military Justice) should begin with a generalized vocabulary of terms that should be known by all NCOs and that once learned, will enhance the rest of the program. A few of these terms are:

- mitigation
- admonition
- reprimand
- redress
- remission
- vacation
- military discipline
- military courtesy
- open hearing
- unsuitable
- appeal
- decision period
- suspension
- setting aside
- non-punitive discipline
- improper command influence
- military justice jurisdiction
- due process
- law of search and seizure
- non-punitive disciplinary measures
- Manual for Courts Martial
- limited-use policy
- line-of-duty determination
- extenuating circumstances

NCOs armed with a complete understanding of these terms and the references from which they come are an asset to the NCO Corps. These few terms will give them the foundation on which they can build additional knowledge of military justice.

UCMJ

Knowledge of the System . . .

NCOs who reach the senior ranks should have acquired a body of knowledge concerning the Uniform Code of Military Justice (UCMJ) mainly because of their involvement in an offense committed by their soldiers along the way, not because of a structured learning process. NCOs in general cannot explain the sources of authority for the military criminal justice system because the program of learning does not focus on specifics, only on general knowledge. Until the NCOs' education system is revamped, the first sergeant must take on the task of ensuring the spirit of the corps is upheld.

The best method that I found was to use a simple vocabulary of military criminal justice terms as the start point. This method activated the thought process. Secondly, this method stimulated an interest to read additional information associated with each single term.

Another method was to have each sergeant in the unit complete a DA Form 2627 (Record of Proceedings Under Article 15, UCMJ). Follow-on to the completing of the form was to explain the various sections of the form and where the information was found.

The program of learning would continue as in this example using AR 27-10, 27-14, AR 600-20 to develop:

NCO Disciplinary Policies . . .

1. NCOs do not have the authority to impose nonjudicial punishment on other enlisted personnel under the UCMJ, Article 15. However, the commander may authorize an NCO in the grade E7 or above, provided such person is senior to the person being notified, to deliver the DA Form 2627 (Record of Proceedings under Article 15, UCMJ) and inform the member of his or her rights.

   In cases of nonjudicial punishment, the recommendations of NCOs should be sought and considered by the unit commanders.

2. As enlisted commanders of soldiers, NCOs are invaluable in furthering the efficiency of the company. This function includes preventing incidents that would make it necessary

to report to trial by court-martial or to impose nonjudicial punishment.

Thus, NCOs are assistants to commanders in administering minor non-punitive discipline as set forth in AR 27-10 and paragraph 1g, part V, MCM.

Non-punitive discipline is not to be confused with nonjudicial punishment.

3. When nonjudicial punishment (UCMJ, Article 15) is imposed on an NCO, it may not include any type of extra duty involving labor or duties not customarily performed by an NCO of the grade and rank of the person who is to perform the extra duty.

Maintenance of Order . . .

1. Army and Marine Corps military police, Air Force security police, and members of the Navy and Coast Guard shore patrols are authorized and directed to apprehend Armed Forces members who commit offenses punishable under the UCMJ.

2. NCOs are authorized and directed to quell all quarrels, frays, and disorders among persons subject to military law and to apprehend participants. Those exercising authority, hereunder, should do so with judgment and tact.

Exercising Military Authority . . .

1. Military authority will be exercised with promptness, firmness, courtesy, and justice. Resorting to trial by court-martial, or to nonjudicial punishment under UCMJ, Article 15, will not be done for trivial offenses, except when less drastic methods of administering discipline have been tried unsuccessfully.

2. One of the most effective non-punitive disciplinary measures is extra training or instruction. If soldiers have a training deficiency, they will be required to take extra training in subjects directly related to that deficiency.

3. The training or instruction given to a soldier to correct deficiencies not only must be directly related to the deficiency observed, but also must be oriented to

improving the soldier's performance in his or her problem area.

Corrective measures may be taken after normal duty hours. Such measures ensure the nature of training or instruction, not punishment.

4. Care should be taken at all levels of command to ensure that training and instruction are not used in an oppressive manner to evade the procedural safeguards applying to imposing nonjudicial punishment.

Relationships of Superiors Toward Subordinates . . .

1. Leaders at all echelons will continuously give troops constructive information on the need for and purpose of military discipline.

   Articles in the UCMJ requiring explanation will be presented in such a way to ensure that soldiers will be fully aware of the controls and obligations imposed on them by virtue and their military service.

2. Commissioned officers and NCOs will keep in close touch with soldiers in their command, take an interest in their organizational life, hear *their complaints*, and work at all times to remove causes for dissatisfaction.

3. Leaders will strive to maintain positive relations with soldiers in their command. To this end, the leader's confidence and sympathy should ensure that the soldiers feel free to approach them for counsel and assistance.

   Ideally, soldiers in their command should feel free to discuss not only military and organizational matters, but personal problems as well, or matters that may contribute to personal or family problems. This relationship may be gained and maintained without relearning discipline.

Complaint . . .

1. A member of the Armed Forces may submit an Article 138 complaint for any act or omission by his commanding officer that he believes to be wrong and for which he has requested redress and been refused.

2. A member who, through no fault of his own, has not received a final response within 10 duty days may elect to treat that as a refusal of redress.
3. Commanders are encouraged to consult with their NCOs on the appropriate type, duration, and limits of punishment to be imposed.
   Additionally, as NCOs are often in the best position to observe a soldier undergoing punishment and evaluate daily performance and attitude, their views on clemency should be given careful consideration.

Effective Date and Execution of Punishments . . .

1. Unsuspended punishments of reduction and forfeiture of pay take effect on the date imposed. Other unsuspended punishments take effect on the date they are imposed, unless the imposing commander prescribes otherwise.
2. In those cases where the execution of the punishment legitimately must be delayed, e.g., the members are hospitalized, placed on quarters, authorized emergency leave, or on brief periods of TDY or a brief field problem, the execution of the punishment should begin immediately thereafter.

Important Areas Covered by Armed Regulation 600-20 . . .

1. Private indebtedness and financial obligations (AR 210-7 and AR 600-15).
2. Settlement of local accounts on change of station.
3. Release of personnel rosters, orders, or similar documents (AR 340-21).
4. Congressional activities (AR 380-5).
5. Participation in pageants and shows for civilian entertainment (AR 360-61, Chap 4).
6. Membership campaigns.
7. Political activities and public demonstrations.
8. Medical care performed with or without the member's permission.

Appeal(s) . . .

1. The member may, pending submission and decision on the appeal, be required to undergo the punishment imposed, but once submitted, such appeal will be promptly decided.
2. If the appeal is not decided within *3 calendar days*, excluding the day of submission, and if the member so requests, further performance of any punishments involving deprivation of liberty will be delayed pending the decision on the appeal.
3. All appeals will be made on DA Form 2627 or DA Form 2627-1 and forwarded through the imposing commander or successor-in-command, when applicable, to the superior authority.
4. The superior authority will act on the appeal unless otherwise directed by competent authority. The member may attach documents to the appeal for consideration.
5. A member is not required to state reasons for his or her appeal; however, the member may do so. For example, the person may state the following in the appeal: a. Based on the evidence, he or she does not believe he or she is guilty. b. The punishment imposed is excessive, or that a certain punishment should be mitigated or suspended.
6. A superior authority will act on the appeal expeditiously, and may conduct an independent inquiry into the case, if necessary or desirable.

Pretrial Confinement . . .

. . . accused still a soldier . . .

Confinement of one of your soldiers falls into the same category as relief for cause in terms of the devastating effects to the soldier's psychological well-being. Much thought must be given to the use of a lesser form of restraint to prevent the accused soldier from engaging in serious criminal misconduct, doing bodily harm to him or herself, or to ensure the accused soldier is present for trial. The accused soldier is still a soldier despite what the command believes, has knowledge of, or concludes. It is important that you continue to treat this soldier as you would any other soldier. Now there are critical job positions that a soldier may hold that will require a temporary change of duty position pending the outcome of the trial. His or her status as the noblest creature on the face of the Earth has not been lost. The soldier still has rights under the Constitution of the United States, whi7ch is the basic authority for the military criminal justice system.

. . . what does the accused do while awaiting trial . . .

The accused soldier pending court martial charges should be allowed to continue the performance of normal duties and responsibilities while awaiting trial. Of course there are some exceptions to that statement, the first sergeant is paid to use good judgment. However, it is suggested that you consider the type of duty performed by the accused, the relationship of the accused soldier with other soldiers, etc. The first sergeant, as the leader has to understand what such an action as changing a soldier's position or ordering confinement does to soldier's self-esteem. In your thoughts, think in favor of the soldier, unless in the best interest of the unit or the Army you have to think otherwise.

. . . best guidance . . .

The best guideline the first sergeant and the commander could use concerning pretrial confinement is contained in the Manual for Courts-Martial, United States 1984, RCM 305, which states that:

> When probable cause exists to believe that a soldier has committed an offense trial be court-martial, he may be placed in pre-trial confinement only if there is probable cause to believe (1) that the accused will not be present for trial, a pre-trial hearing, or investigation, or (2) the accused will engage in serious criminal misconduct, and (3) less severe forms of restraint are inadequate to ensure the accused presence or prevent his serious criminal misconduct.

. . . reasons to confine . . .

Serious criminal misconduct includes intimidation of witnesses, obstruction of justice, seriously injuring others, or other offenses that pose a serious threat to the safety of the community, or to the effectiveness, morale, discipline, readiness, or safety of the command, or to the national security of the United States.

... to confine or not to confine ...

A person should not be confined as a mere matter of convenience or expedience. In deciding whether or not confinement is necessary, consider these factors:

a. nature and circumstances of the offenses charged or suspected, including extenuating circumstances;
b. weight of the evidence against the accused;
c. accused's ties to the local, including family, off-duty employment, financial resources, and length of residence;
d. accused's character and mental conditions (psychological state);
e. accused's service record, including any record of previous misconduct;
f. accused's record of appearance at or flight from other pretrial investigations, trials, and similar proceedings; and
g. likelihood that the accused can and will commit further serious criminal misconduct if allowed to remain at liberty (based on the known conduct of the accused).

Improper Command Influence ...

... overstepping military justice boundaries ...

Occasionally leaders project far beyond the responsibilities and duties of military justice. By overstepping these boundaries, they violate the purpose of military criminal law, that of promoting justice, assisting in and maintaining good order and discipline, and promoting effectiveness and efficiency.

... prohibition as applied to rank or stages of process ...

Article 37, Uniform Code of Military Justice, prohibits improper command influence. There is no sanction for any rank or grade who violates this article. The prohibition of improper command influence applies to all stages of the military judicial process. Some examples, and there are many, would be the use of rank or position to intimidate witnesses or the accused soldier or obstruction of justice by holding up the military judicial process for no apparent reason(s).

The Staff Judge Advocate (SJA) should always be contacted when there are questions concerning matters that may affect the administration of the military judicial process.

... yardstick to court-martial ...

A soldier has the right to refuse an Article 15, DA Form 2627 (Record of Proceedings Under Article 15, UCMJ) (unless attached to or embarked on a ship) and demand trial by court-martial. This, of course, is done after the commander informs the accused soldier of his or her legal rights and the soldier is given a reasonable amount of time to see a military lawyer (civilian lawyer at the soldier's expense). Another consideration for nonjudicial punishment should be sufficient evidence to support a conviction if the accused soldier refuses the Article 15 and demands a trial by court-martial.

If the accused soldier has committed an offense made punishable by one of the punitive articles, Articles 77-134, of the UCMJ and there is sufficient evidence, then proceed with the nonjudicial punishment. Every case will not require punitive action.

Personnel Appearance at the Trial ...

... representing their unit ...

The witnesses, the escort (if required), the accused soldier, and the subordinate leaders of these soldiers will be reminded that the Army is a uniformed service where discipline is judged, in part, by the manner in which they wear the uniform as prescribed by AR 670-1. Once the unit has been notified by the trial counsel of the time and place of the trial and the names of the witnesses required for the Government or the defense, these soldiers should be inspected to ensure a neat and well-groomed appearance. You should further ensure that all designated witnesses are in a clean and complete Class A uniform with insignia of grade, authorized ribbons/awards and proper patches. These soldiers will be representing their unit—your unit.

Escort ...

... additional requirements if confinement is adjudged ...

The guilty finding of the accused soldier where confinement may be adjudged, or where the accused soldier has been placed in pre-trial confinement, will require an escort (a prisoner guard) and the necessary transportation to escort the accused soldier from place of trial to place of confinement. Consider these general guidelines in the selection of an escort. The escort should:

1. Be of sound character and ready psychologically to take on the mission.
2. Be qualified with the weapon used in the performance of the duty (if required to be armed). This means that you must look at qualifying personnel other than the seniors.
3. Be in the grade of sergeant (E5) or higher.
4. Be in grade equal to or senior to that of the accused soldier.

The trial counsel will provide the escort instructions such as:

1. Arrival time and designated time of the trial.
2. Instructions not to allow the prisoner out of sight and custody until the accused is duly delivered to the appropriate confinement authority.

Diamond Point: When the above tasks are not well planned, your stress level will be high. Ensure that you give the escort a good, solid brief on the importance of guarding a prisoner.

Points to Ponder . . .

1. First Sergeant understands that a superior authority over the officer who imposed the punishment may review cases whether or not an appeal is filed by the defendant. The reason the superior officer would want to review the case is what's important. Talk to your CSM about such case reviews (good senior level NCODP).
2. For soldiers pending criminal investigation on charges who are within 40 days or so of release from active duty, you must ensure that the area's Staff Judge Advocate (SJA) is notified expeditiously.

... consider these measures ...

3. A request for administrative hold through the SJA's office to the MILPO if a witness might receive a permanent change of station orders (PCS), be transferred, be gone on an extended TDY, or have a school date before or during the time of trial. Coordination must be made with all elements concerned.

   a. Transportation
   b. Redeployment Section
   c. Personnel Management Section
   d. The Accused's Unit Commander (and 1SG)
   e. The Witness' Unit Commander (and 1SG)

4. The request for administrative hold should contain the following information:

   a. Witness Prospective Reassignment
   b. The case for which the testimony is required
   c. The date(s) witness is required

5. A specified duty of the unit commander, responsibility to ensure the presence of the accused for trial or any other administrative action, is an implied duty of the first sergeant.

6. Once your unit is notified of the time and place of the names of witnesses, establish a unit point of contact, i.e., the platoon sergeant of the witness(es), to ensure the following:

   a. Complete and clean Class A uniform.
   b. Witnesses do not perform duties the day before the trial, i.e., CQ, guard duty.
   c. Needed transportation is provided.
   d. Meal card holders have their meal cards in their possession.
   e. Escorts detailed from your unit should:

      (1) Be in appropriate seasonal Class A uniform.
      (2) Be of equal or senior in grade.

        (3)   Be an E-5 or above.

        (4)   Will be instructed to ensure understanding of the importance of this duty.

           a.   Will not allow the prisoner to go anywhere alone.

           b.   Will ensure that the prisoner is allowed to eat at prescribed times.

           c.   Report all and any problems encountered.

f.   Place all potential court-martial witnesses in an on-call status, i.e., no passes, TDY orders, schools, or ordinary leave. For those potential witnesses, emergency leave should not be allowed until contact has been made with the SJA.

g.   The CSM should be personally notified at any time of an incident that may result in a criminal investigations, letters of reprimand, or any disciplinary action involving a senior NCO.

h.   Immediately report confinement of your soldiers by civilian authorities to the next higher headquarter.

i.   Ensure that witnesses understand the importance of the role they will play in this judicial process. They must be instructed that their actions or lack thereof could result in dismissal of the pending charges against the defendant.

Diamond Point #1: You must coordinate requests for administrative hold with AG Personnel Records Section, Personnel Management Section, or Redeployment Section.

Diamond Point #2: Notify the SJA in all cases of soldiers pending criminal charges or investigation who are within 30-45 days of their release from active duty.

Disciplinary Infractions (Minor) . . .

. . . dealing with disciplinary growing pains . . .

Soldiers enter the military with various levels of instilled discipline that comes from various sources. Most of them immediately apply that discipline that life has given them, however, others have trouble breaking the discipline code. Most soldiers go through their entire career and never present any disciplinary infractions They always obey the lawful orders of the superiors appointed over them. For others, the growing pains continue from one trivial offense to another. These soldiers become leadership distractors.

Disciplinary infractions, however minor, must be dealt with. Some questions must be answered to ensure that your unit's leadership groups understand the intention of dealing with minor infractions. The questions concerning minor infractions are:

1. How many times must the same minor infraction be committed by the same soldier within a reasonable period before it is moved to the major infraction category?

2. Does the subordinate leader keep some kind of record of the soldier's minor infractions in order to present a credible case when nonjudicial punishment is requested by the leader?

3. How many times does the soldier have to show up late for a formation or duty, fail to respond to the first call in the morning, fail to be at an appointed place of duty at an appointed time, fail to take pride in military appearance and physical fitness, or fail to control personal affairs before punitive action is taken?

4. How and when will the documents used to counsel the soldier who has committed minor disciplinary infractions be referred for chapter action under the provision of AR 635-200?

5. When should the soldier's file be elevated to a higher level in the chain of command for review?

6. Do the subordinate leaders know the document requirement for command referral and review, i.e., rehabilitation efforts statements, outside agency involvement, etc.?

7. Do the subordinate leaders know how to prepare a brief written memorandum explaining requested actions?

8. Should the first sergeant maintain a "Special Attention" file for those soldiers on the edge of separation under the provision of AR 635-200?

. . . all infractions require prompt action . . .

The actions taken for minor disciplinary infractions require the same degree of promptness as would a major infraction. Justice is not served by delays of action. The soldier deserves to be informed of the infraction, the action requested, and when results of requested action can be expected. Speedy disposition also helps promote good morale and discipline.

CHAPTER VII

VOCABULARY

While this vocabulary may or may not agree with Webster, these concepts are to be developed by future enlightened enlisted leaders of America. Is there a document that states that we enlisted cannot have our own specific vocabulary? I will be asked often why I did not put the vocabulary in alphabetical order. The only answer is that you should not want everything to come to you easily. For in challenge is progress, reward, and accomplishment.

Recrimination—to oppose one accusation with another.

Agenda—a list of things to be done, especially the program for a meeting.

Open Agenda—having no limit on life involvement or interaction with soldiers and family members.

Closed Agenda—having a limit on how much you will allow the elements of your personal life to interfere with your military progress. This includes all aspects of a person's life. The closed agenda is usually not openly declared. Positions of leadership require that the closed agenda be greatly decreased in relationship with the open agenda as one rises in the ranks.

Confidante—one to whom secrets or private matters are confided.

Dysfunctional stress—when stressful elements, action requirements, rules, or activities cause disorder or impaired functioning.

Organizational Life—the soldier's environment (internal and external to unit life). This includes physical facilities, health and dental facilities, community facilities, but it reaches far deeper than these things. Organizational life includes, but is not limited to, the soldier response to these elements; the soldier's ability to adapt to these elements; the soldier's willingness to adapt or respond; the soldier's participation; and most importantly, the soldier's ability (as authorized by the command) to effect changes in his or her own environment.

Diamond Point: effort to further clarify, define, make clear, or modify already stated fact(s).

Exaggerated Fears: that which frightens off prospective first sergeants who are not totally committed to anything or anyone other than himself or herself. The effects of being told of the burden that is placed on the first sergeants shoulders, the continuous requirements, and the extended hours.

Program of Learning—a method of determining what needs to be learned concerning any subject, in which sequence it should be learned, how long it should take to complete a certain subject, and who should be required to learn the subject.

Solidifying Element—that element in any organization who is first to understand the internal organizational aspects of the past and the present and is able to use that knowledge to unify the organization.

Premeditated Mental Activation—mentally activating yourself, before you pin on the diamond, and tasks to be required of you as 1SG. Preparing mentally for any task, mentally, physically, spiritually, or psychologically.

Convert—to persuade or induce to adopt a particular religion, faith, or belief, to change from one use, function, or purpose to another; adapt to a new or different purpose.

Usurer—a person who lends money at an exorbitant or unlawful rate of interest.

Usurious—practicing usury.

Usury—the act or practice of lending money at an exorbitant or illegal rate of interest.

Transition Interaction Integration—the process a new member of an organization must go through to become a part of the spirit of that element. Because the Army is an ever-moving and-changing organization, assimilating into a unit should not be a complex occurrence. Soldiers must quickly pick up the step by interacting with all elements as soon as possible to become effective members. (Sponsorship)

Prodigy—a person or thing so extraordinary as to inspire wonder.

Phenomenon—anything extremely unusual.

Bottoms-Up-Training-Identification—identifying those tasks for training that the squad leader and the squad leader alone decides what should go on the training schedule.

Warfighting Molding Process—a mental process of getting all leaders to understand what the requirements of war are really all about. Once leaders understand the requirements, they then ensure that all that they do involves that understanding. The molding questions associated with this process sound like these:

- Why is the mental process of discipline so very important to a soldier?
- Do I as the leader bear the death of a soldier who goes into combat ill trained?
- Is the fact that my soldiers might not like me because of my tough training really one of my leadership concerns?

Specialization Attunement—providing your expert attention to a limited number of subjects. It also intensifies the need for directing, planning, controlling, or coordinating various specialized activities at your level to overcome the limits.

Improper Command Influence—the actions and/or recommendations of a commander on nonjudicial punishment or trial by court-martialmust represent the commander's independent judgement uninfluenced by the belief that the desires of a superior commander are being complied with.

Warfighting Readiness—creating a firm understanding within the entire unit that war is a "come as you are" event. Be ye also ready—for you know not the day nor the hour.

Clique—(coalitions, triads) authorized or unauthorized, supported or unsupported, they are counter-productive to good order and are not in keeping with the spirit of the chain of command. Destroy them on site and do not allow their rebirth; be ye known as a clique booster.

First Sergeant Intent—the concept that the next qualified leader understands that the train does not stop or slow down in the absence of the 1SG.

Human Automation—subordinates give only what is asked, or less, all according to what button is pressed. The soldier does nothing beyond what is required.

Immoderate Language—verbal condemnation, vulgar speech, profane or obscene language that causes resentment and friction in the ranks. Sarcasm and irony that could leave soldiers in doubt as to exactly what the leader means also falls into this category.

Bottoms-up Training—training initiated from the bottom of the chain (section chief, squad leader). E.g., I know that three of my soldiers need to qualify with their weapon. I will ensure the training NCO schedules them for the range. See also bottoms-up-training-identification.

Tops-down Training—training initiated by elements at the top of the chain for lower elements.

Condor Leader—peers from everywhere and anywhere and at all hours of the day and night, recording all human frailties with the emphasis on the failures of those he or she leads.

Sense of Comradeship—a philosophy that must be preached by all first sergeant because all NCOs share common goals and objectives, they must support each other to the maximum extent to ensure mission accomplishment. They must share experiences in their learning. When one NCO fails to complete a mission, it is a failure for the entire NCO Corps. Dereliction by one is shared by all.

Military Judicial Process—in addition to what it means as seen through the eyes of the commander, of the Staff Judge Advocate, the NCO Corps must study the concepts and prescribed policies governing the administration of military justice. NCOs, by having this knowledge at their command, will be able to better support the concept of discipline and good order.

Words or Phrases Explained

Trained to Train—understanding the principles of training that ensure that the trainer does not compromise the training plan. Understanding that at the end of the training session the student must be smarter than he was before the session.

Sacred Trust—the belief that those things entrusted to us in leadership take on a significance just below that sacredness we find in church. Worthy of respect.

Point of the Bayonet—any danger that our soldiers could be confronted with in terms of battlefield sustainment or battlefield lethality. Soldier's lives on the line.

Test of Leadership Stamina—being presented with, confronted by, demanded, or commanded to some veritable conglomeration of things, people, and considerations within the course of the few hours the leader has to deal with problems, difficulties and unpopular decisions.

Skill Decay—degradation of skills has no respect for grade levels or rank.

Dereliction—neglect of duty or obligation. Willful neglect, as of duty.

Hats—moods you adapt to deal with various situations. The wearing of these hats is the result of some frustrating event(s) stimulating some type of behavior.

. . . teaching hat—imparting knowledge to a subordinate in other than a threatening mood.

. . . ass-chewing hat (negativism, hostility, striking out, snide remarks)

. . . subordinate leader's hat—taking some action away from a subordinate leader that is clearly within the subordinate leader's scope.

Discipline Breaches:

Breach—the act or offense of failing to keep the law or to do what the law, duty, or obligation requires.

Dereliction, delinquency, neglect, disregard, infraction, trespass, contravention, transgression, violation

       ★   Training Breaches
       ★   Management Breach
       ★   Command Breach

★   Leadership Breach
★   Quality-of-Life Breach
★   Standards Breach
★   Competency Breach

Philosopher—Kings (Plato) Thought

- would never act out of ignorance or prejudice;
- would never be pushed into making a bad decision;
- would never be more interested in power, money, or an NCOER or OER rating than a soldier's welfare.

Pre-Position Mental Activation Process—mental process of determining what the duty should entail before assuming the duty.

Post-Position Mental Activation Process—mental process of what life after 1SG duty should entail.

Mastered Moral Distinctions

- distinguishing right from wrong at all levels
- improper request from seniors

Micro-Challenges—that conglomeration of things, people, or considerations to which you commit time and effort, but are challenges that could very well be handled by a subordinate leader.

Demography—study of the vital statistics of human populations, as size, growth, density, and distribution.

Indiscipline Rates—AWOL, Articles 15, drug and alcohol abuse incidents, child or spouse abuse, disrespect to NCOs, theft, etc.

Tactical Competency—properly qualified, capable, adequately trained to perform that tactically as well as to be able to train tactics.

Spirit To Achieve Successful Training—accepting the challenges of training, the determination to do the best job possible, the sincere zeal and interest shown in preparation and execution of training and capitalizing on the outcome.

Specified Duties—duties with which a soldier is charged in Department of the Army or Department of Defense publications. Always in writing in any authorized military media such as policy letter or statement, memorandum, MOU, LOIs, general orders, UCMJ, etc., and directed at a specific job.

Implied Duties—unlike those duties specifically stated in a Department of the Army or Department of Defense publication (specified duty), or unlike those duties that meet specific requirements and may be given verbally (directed duties), these duties carry a very distinct characteristic, the amount of individual soldiers' control over these fundamental duties that are essential to the day-to-day effectiveness of the Army. These unwritten duties support the other duties.

Informal Contract—consists of those implied obligations and responsibilities that the organization and the soldier have to each other. The informal contract is based on individual and organizational expectations and on the necessity for each to satisfy the other (FM 22-100, June 1973).

TIMES TO REMEMBER AS
A FIRST SERGEANT

TIME TO REMEMBER AS A FIRST SERGEANT

Date:
Remarks:

Date:
Remarks:

Date:
Remarks:

Date:
Remarks:

ADDITIONAL READING
FOR SUCCESS

◊ DA PAM 600-24, Suicide Prevention and Psychological Autopsy.
◊ DA PAM 27-50-102, The Army Lawyer.
◊ FM 22-5, Drill and Ceremonies. Provides guidance for Army-wide uniformity in the conduct of drill and ceremonies.
◊ FM 22-100, Military Leadership. Provides an overview of Army leadership doctrine, including principles for applying leadership theory at all organizational levels to meet operational requirements.
◊ AR 600-20, Army Command Policy and Procedures. Prescribes guidance covering military discipline and conduct, proceeding of rank, and the military Equal Opportunity (EO) Program.
◊ DOD Regulation 5500.7-R, Joint Ethics Regulation Standards of Conduct for Department of the DOD Personnel. Prescribes standards of conduct required of all DOD personnel, regardless of assignment to avoid conflicts and the appearance of conflict between private interests and official duties.
◊ AR 601-280, Total Army Retention Program. Prescribes uniform procedures for immediate reenlistment or extension of expiration of term of service (ETS) of those soldiers serving in the Active Army.
◊ AR 635-200, Personnel Separations, Enlisted Personnel, 17 Oct 1990. Prescribes policies, standards, and procedures to ensure the readiness and competency of the force while providing for the orderly administrative separation of soldiers for a variety of reasons.
◊ AR 840-10, Heraldic Activities, Flags, Guidons, Streamers, Tabards, and Automobile and Aircraft Plates, 1 October 1979. Prescribes the design, acquisition display, and use of flags, guidons, streamers, automobile, and aircraft paltes, and tabors by DA organizations and personnel.
◊ FM 25-101, (Training The Force) Battle Focused Training, September 20. Helps the leader to focus on realistic training as well as on demanding training.

◊   AR 623-205, Noncommissioned Officer Evaluation Reporting System. Contains instructions for preparing, processing and submitting DA Form 2166-8 (Noncommissioned Officer Evaluation Report (NCO-ER).

◊   AR 672-5-1, Military Awards. Prescribes policy, criteria to provide tangible recognition for acts of valor, exceptional service or achievement, special skills or qualifications, acts of heroism not involving actual combat.

◊   AR 600-200, Enlisted Personnel Management System. Prescribes policies and procedures for career management, classification, and reclassification in a military occupational specialty, utilization, administering special-duty assignment (proficiency pay), promotions, and reductions in rank and testing Active Army enlisted soldiers.

REFERENCES

★ FM 27-14, Legal Guide for Soldiers
★ AR 27-10, Military Justice
★ AR 600-15, Indebtedness of Military Personnel
★ AR 600-20, Army Command Policy and Procedures
★ AR 608-99, Family Support, Child Custody, and Paternity
★ AR 608-47
★ AR 350 Series
★ AR 635-200, Personnel Separations, Enlisted Personnel
★ AR 690-500, Civilian Position Management
★ Manual for Courts-Martial, United States, 1984
★ DA Pam 600-19, Quality of Life
★ FM 25-2
★ FM 25-100, Training the Force
★ FM 25-101, Training the Force, Battle Focused Training
★ Forms or Documents Cited:
  - DA Form 2627, (Record of Proceedings Under Article 15, UCMJ)
  - DA Form 2166-8, NCO Evaluation Report (NCO-ER)
  - DA Form 2166-8-1, NCO Counseling Checklist/Record

ABOUT THE AUTHOR

Sergeant Major (R) Owens, a native of Memphis, Tennessee, held every enlisted leadership position from squad leader to first sergeant. He was both a battalion and brigade command sergeant major.

His military schooling included instructor training, NCO Academy, ANCOC, Criterion Instructor Workshop, Leadership and Management Development Course, NCOLP and the United States Army Sergeants Major Academy—Class 22.

INDEX

A

Armed Forces Officer, The 78, 83, 84, 134
artificial dissemination 36
AWOL (absent without leave) 76, 93,
  98, 102, 204

B

bar to reenlist (BTR) 42, 47, 55, 86,
  133, 160
Byzantines 11, 134

C

change of command 52, 74, 116, 129
  checklist 129
combat effectiveness indicators 23, 27,
  28, 38, 46, 101, 104, 132, 160, 167
command climate 19, 43, 47, 78, 82,
  163
complex leadership 18
counseling 20, 70, 92, 95, 99, 103,
  121, 123, 124, 125, 126, 133, 136,
  142, 144, 149, 150, 154, 160, 211
  debt 54
  face-to-face 125, 126
  framework for 107
  initial 125
  NCOER form 125
  negative 149, 150
  professional 91
  scope of 95
court-martial 183, 191
court-martial, trial by. *See*
  punishment, nonjudicial

D

disciplinary infractions, minor 34,
  197, 198
  dealing with 196, 197
diversified American culture 82, 110
DOD Regulation 5500.7-R, Joint
  Ethics Regulation 40, 42, 46, 103,
  143, 144, 145, 209
DVO Model 63, 72, 73

E

Ethics Regulation. *See* DOD
  Regulation 5500.7-R, Joint Ethics
  Regulation
ethnic observances 42, 48, 64, 82,
  101, 103, 107, 110, 112

F

face-to-face initial counseling 125, 126
falling on your sword 134
Family Support Agenda (FSA) 65,
  103, 153
Family Support Group (FSG) 33, 39,
  40, 41, 46, 48, 59, 64, 67, 73, 74,
  75, 94
framework
  for development 112
  for evaluation 113
  for leadership 18, 21, 32, 76, 81, 104,
    105, 106, 107, 108, 109, 110,
    118, 136, 157, 158, 161
  for spouse learning 70
  of learning 32, 81, 128

215